2 Commas In 2 Years:
Practical, Step by Step Methods to Making Your First Million Online

2 Commas In 2 Years

2 Commas In 2 Years:
Practical, Step by Step Methods to Making Your First Million Online

Neema Imantabari

nPublishing

2 Commas In 2 Years

2 Commas In 2 Years

Practical, Step by Step Methods to Making Your First Million Online

First Printing: 2017

ISBN: 978-1543017779

nPublishing Limited

imantabari.com

neema@neemaimantabari.com

First Edition

"If I had asked people what they wanted, they would have said faster horses." – Henry Ford.

This book is dedicated to those who use their time, money and power for good.

Neema Imantabari

Contents

Neema Imantabari

Preface

The inspiration for this book came after, seeing all these "internet guru's" selling thousand dollar programs on how to make money online when the only way they make money is teaching others how to make money. After doing some Google searches, I once again found nothing of value and found no actually methods that could make any money online that were legitimate, by someone who has been there and done it.

As someone who has been in your position, I understand the struggle, and I am here to help. This book was written to help people achieve financial freedom, by sharing real and practical methods you can use to make money. This book is for anyone looking to make more money, whether you are just starting out or an advanced internet marketer who wants to scale their business and add additional income streams.

To keep this book as authentic as possible, I have refrained from hiring an editor, so please forgive me for this books' lack of impressive words, economic facts and at times, poor grammar – I aim to create millionaires from this book, not award-winning writers or economists. I want to help every person reading this to achieve financial freedom, I ask only of two things in return:

1. You will help other's (whether it be through time, money, or knowledge).

2. You will keep this book until you make your first million – and will make me the first to know about it.

Today's Date 16/08/20'   **Signed:**

2 Commas In 2 Years

Introduction

I was a broke 13-year-old kid, that wanted to make money but had no idea where to start. I would Google 'how to become a millionaire' but was faced with the same problem... there were no practical methods to make money online, I would only be confronted with pages, and pages of motivational advice telling me I could do it or even worse, people trying to sell their £5000 courses, telling me how to make money is making courses teaching others how to make money or completing surveys.

After years of trying just about every method to making money online, I want to share with you the best methods I have found. Why would I do this since there is little to no money in writing books? I want to help others by teaching exactly what I wanted to know when first starting out, to save you time and money. The methods I am going to share have created multiple income streams and a digital marketing agency that has helped hundreds of businesses. There is no theory in this book, everything you learn can be directly used to make money.

I promise you, becoming a millionaire is not that of fantasy or only for those that come from wealthy families. To put it into perspective how easy it is to make a million, let's do some basic math.

> Here are a few ways to a £1,000,000:
>
> - Salary £50k x 20 years.
>
> - Salary £100k x 10 years.
>
> - Earn £114 per hour, every hour of the year.
>
> - 2,000 people buy a £500 product.
>
> - 5,000 people buy a £200 product.
>
> - 1,000 people buy a £1000 product.
>
> - 10,000 people buy a £100 product.
>
> - 300 people pay £278 per month for 12 months.
>
> - 1,000 people pay £83 a month for 12 months.
>
> - 5000 people pay £8.50 per month for 24 months.

Only when you remove your limiting beliefs as to why you cannot achieve the million, is when you can achieve it. Ask yourself the following:

1. Is there £1,000,000 on the planet? Yes / No.

2. Who has your money? _____

3. What do you need to do to collect it? _____

Use math to create possibility, and allow my methods to add strategy on how you will achieve your first million and beyond.

How to Increase Your Net Worth

I recommend that you track and document your finances since most of the methods are purely online, it is easy to think money is not real. Let's calculate your current net worth and its' contributors. You can't make a million if you aren't worth a million.

Influence

How many people can you reach? (in person, on social media etc.)

_____

How will you increase this number starting today?

_____
_____
_____

Health

How would you describe your physical health?

_____

How do you wish to improve your health starting today?

_____
_____
_____

Skills

What skills do you have? (e.g. can you code, can you cook well etc.)

_____
_____
_____

What skill do you wish to learn / master?

_____

_____

How will you start to master that skill starting today?

_____

_____

Pure Finance

What was your active income last month? (money you had to work for).

_____

What was your passive income last month? (money that came into your account with little effort).

_____

Total income last month?

_____

How could you increase your income?

_____

_____

Invested

How much money do you have invested and in what?

_____

How much do you have in short-term investments? (0-12 months).

_____

How much do you have in mid-term investments? (1-10 years).

_____

How much do you have in long-term investments? (10+ years).

_____

Where could you invest your money with little risk?

_____

Liabilities

Your total money spent last month?

_____

How could you save an extra 25% every month?

_____

_____

_____

Total money made last month – total money spent

_____

Please complete this every month for the following 24 months to track your progress.

How to Use This Book

Before we go any further, understand that I do not wish to waste your time by delving deep into detail on anything you can find with a quick Google search or a typical business/self-help book talking about mindsets of success or the basics of learning a skill. I expect you to research every topic discussed – if you want to monetize this book to its full potential.

"You can make money or excuses. Your choice." – John Addison.

This book contains everything you need to make millions – if there is something you need to learn about that is not mentioned in this book such as growing your social media accounts, learning how to code or ranking websites to the top of Google, you can Google how. There are no methods in this book that require you to pay for something elsewhere to learn – everything you need to know is on Google and Youtube for free. If you don't know what a word means – Google it, if you are too lazy to do that, you will never become a millionaire anyway. So, with the small rant over – let's make millions!

Neema Imantabari

Making Your Start-Up Money

When you don't have money, you have time.
And when you have time, you can make money, just
add strategy and effort. – Neema Imantabari.

Making Your Initial Start-Up Money

Your first step is to raise money to finance your businesses, even if you have the funds to finance your business, follow the start-up money advice since you can make some good money with little effort through selling your unused items.

You have two options for raising your initial start-up money:

1. You could get a full time/part time job and work on your business after working hours until you starting making enough where you can quit your job and make a solid, stable income.

2. I guarantee you that you have at least £500-5000 worth of junk and unused items, whether it be books, clothes, games or toys that you will be able to sell on eBay (or any other marketplace).

Now you have the initial money to start your business we can progress to the step by step methods that will enable you to make your first million. I highly suggest using many of these methods and businesses in conjunction; it is essential to have multiple cash flows, it is estimated that the average millionaire has 7 income streams. Your target with these income streams is to create such profitable streams that if all but one of your income streams stop, the final one will keep you covered.

Arbitrage

"Don't stay in bed, unless you can make money in bed." – George Burns.

This section is probably the least attractive of all the sections since it requires hard work. Nevertheless, these methods are great for people who are starting out with no skills, that just want to make some money on the side (or even a full-time) income, since these methods do not require a huge investment of time or money.

Arbitrage Using eBay / Amazon

For this method, you will be finding items at charity shops, pound stores, and car boot sales and flipping them for more online, on eBay / Etsy / Amazon.

Visit a place where you can find something for a very good price (e.g. car boot sales/pound shops or a charity shop).

Search for items that are at a very good price and while you are there search for how much that product is being sold on eBay. Make sure when looking through how much the item is being sold for, you do not go on listed items, but sold items. This is so you know yours will sell since it is consistently selling for a price above that of what you bought it. There are now even barcode scanners you could use, to directly scan the product to see how much it is being sold for online. As you start spending more time, you will understand how much different items sell for.

Some great items you could consider flipping are:

- Magazines / Newspapers / Books.
- Toys.
- Phone Accessories / Cases.
- Games.
- Artwork.
- Antique Objects.
- Vintage Clothing.

You could even find items on eBay and sell them for more on Amazon, or hunt for great offers online and resell them if you are patient enough for more. Domains, websites, apps and gaming accounts are easy to flip using websites such as flippa.com and swappa.com if you know the market.

Avira

For this method, you will be selling keys to the popular Antivirus software, Avira.

1. You will need to buy keys for under $8 a key on G2A. Simply google 'g2a Avira antivirus' and search for keys being sold under $8.

2. Your next stop is to create a PayPal account and link it with your eBay account.

3. What you will be doing is buying these keys from G2A and selling them for $15-20 on eBay each. Yes, that easily, you can make $30-80 extra a day.

Currency Exchanging

On many forums and websites, you can currency exchange cryptocurrencies and make money off it by buying low and selling high. Crypto-currency (the most popular being bitcoin) is a decentralised digital currency, that is not regulated (don't worry, it is legal). For this method, we will focus on buying the crypto-currency at a low price and selling for an additional 10%.

For this method, you will need:
- A Coinbase account.
- A Blockchain account.
- A local bitcoin account or eBay account.
- A debit card.
- A verified PayPal or business PayPal account.
- An investment of $50 or more.
- An account on a forum which allows currency exchanges (e.g. bitcointalk.org) / eBay / Local Bitcoin account.

Now you have all the above set up; you are good to go:

1. Start off by purchasing $50 or more worth of Bitcoin on Coinbase with your debit card. The reason for this is that Coinbase has a very low rate when buying bitcoin (around 3%).

2. Your next step after you purchase the bitcoin is to transfer your bitcoin to your Blockchain wallet or local bitcoin account. Now your money is in a different wallet, you can start the exchanging process.

3. You should be looking to exchange at a 15% rate. For example, if I am selling $100 bitcoin, I would want $115 in PayPal for it. Yes, that is around $11 straight up profit if you factor in fees from blockchain and PayPal.

4. The places you can sell for profit are local bitcoin, any forum that allows 'currency exchange' and eBay. Your next step is to make an account on whichever website you decide you want to flip on, you will need to grow a reputation by doing deals, and start increasing your rates once you start to gain a reputation as a trusted exchanger.

You should never deal with anyone with any scam report or bad reputation, because as you may or may not know, you can chargeback PayPal payments, unlike bitcoin transactions, so do your research beforehand. Also, never go first to any user unless they seem extremely trusted and use a middleman since bitcoin is not reversible.

PayPal is known for quickly limiting your account if you break their Terms of Service. For that reason, you might want to opt for another payment which is not PayPal; on local bitcoin, many people do the same and buy bitcoin with bank transfers, which in general is much safer as long as you ask for ID to prove they are the real owner.

Here is a forum in which I exchange on, with my rates shown below, and the real-time price of bitcoin, and how much it is selling on local bitcoin for.

Rate

Selling my BTC for your PP at a 15% rate.

Buying your BTC for my PP at 1:1.

Selling my BTC for Natwest/RBS 'Get Cash Code' at 11%. (No ID required.)

Selling my BTC for UK bank transfer at 13%. (Will need full ID).

Buying UK AGC for PP at 65%, cards must be legally obtained.

1	BTC ▾	=	811.9	GBP ▾

Exchange rate calculated using USD Bitcoin price.

		GBP	GBP
blumanchu (30+; 100%)	Cash deposit: Santander / RBS / Nationwide	1002.22 GBP	100 - 1057 GBP	Buy
vtecboy (1000+; 100%)	Other online payment: ★★ [NO ID] Natwest/RBS ATM "Get Cash" ★★ ✓✓✓	1004.76 GBP	70 - 130 GBP	Buy
orpsy (1000+; 100%)	Cash deposit: Nationwide/YorkshirBank/Santander/Natwest/Barclays	1004.76 GBP	100 - 1630 GBP	Buy
blumanchu (30+; 100%)	National bank transfer: United Kingdom	1010.37	200 - 1066	Buy

You may be thinking why someone would sell to me at 1:1 and why someone would buy it for 15%, this is purely down to reputation. Once you build a reputation anywhere, people are willing to pay a premium since they do not want to risk losing all their money to someone who chargebacks payments. If you want to sell other crypto-currencies other than bitcoin on a website such as eBay, you should purchase your bitcoin and use 'shapeshift' to transfer your bitcoin into another crypto-currency such as ethereum.

In short, you buy bitcoin at 1% and sell for 10-15% and keep the profits, just make sure you deal with legitimate people who will have something to lose. Some places where you can sell your crypto-currency for +15% are eBay, Local Bitcoin, and forums.

Providing a Service

"Change your focus from making money to serving more people. Serving people makes the money come in." – Robert Kiyosaki.

In this section, you will learn how and where to provide a service. Firstly, you will need to pick a skillset and spend time crafting and becoming an expert in that, whether that is programming or graphics design, it doesn't matter. Too many people try to master everything and end up mastering nothing as a result. Hone your one skill to become the best in your field and start a service. I suggest you do not advertise your service until you are truly experienced and good at it, as your reputation will follow you. There are ten-thousand places and ways to promote your service, whether you want to have your own website or use others websites and forums.

Here are some suggestions for services you can run:
- **Programming** – learn how to code and create websites and software for clients.
- **Graphics** – learn how to use Photoshop and create beautiful designs.
- **SEO** – You can learn how search engine optimisation works and approach businesses / create a website showing how you can increase the sales and rank on Google for any business.
- **Security Testing** – Learn how to penetration test websites, acting as a white hat ethical hacker working with website and software owners making sure their websites are secure.
- **Proof-Reading** – edit people's articles, books or blog posts correcting their grammar.
- **Voice Over** – Create voice-overs for people looking for a voice over.

Some of the following are websites where you can advertise your services:

- Fiverr
- SEOClerks
- Freelancer
- UpWork
- Guru
- Toptal
- Konker
- 99designs
- GetACoder
- Elance

There are hundreds of others, all you have to do is search, not to mention forums which you can be involved in and sell your services there.

There are thousands of services you can provide. I suggest always having a website for your service and advertising on forums / in person and on general websites.

I would also always use social media to promote and showcase my work. Even if you do not want to pay money to promote yourself through Facebook/Instagram Ads or influencers, it still provides organic reach. If you provide an excellent service to your customers, they will be sure to promote you and you will be able to find potential customers through organic posts with hashtags. Simply put your website or Fiverr gig in your bio, and you might see an increase in customers.

I suggest starting off with Fiverr, the most popular freelance website. There is a lot of competition on Fiverr, however, there are also a lot of customers. You can transfer this idea to any other freelancing site however. Let's go into detail on how you can get started on Fiverr:

Create an account on fiverr.com and choose which niche you want to go into. You have a choice of just about anything, from voiceovers to editing videos, to coding, to logo designs and everything else in between. You can learn just about anything on YouTube, google or in books on your chosen topic, let's take logo design for our example.

1. Build up a nice portfolio, work for free at the start if you need to.
2. Post your graphic designs on Instagram.
3. Create an account on freelance sites such as Fiverr and forums.
4. Create a gig on Fiverr / forums showing your previous work and start to charge money for graphic design.

Here are 55 niches that you can enter on Fiverr:

1. **3D Book Mock-up** - You don't have to be a graphic designer or Photoshop genius to be able to create a great book mockup. You can find a lot of templates on Graphic River but you must be careful with their usage and licenses. You can also Google book templates.

2. **T-Shirt Mock-up** - You can find free t-shirt mockup templates on pixeden, or any other site if you google it.

3. **Product/Packaging Mockup** – Google 'TechClient product packaging mockup free' and you will find free product packaging templates.

4. **Website Mockup** - There are templates on the internet that can mockup a website by displaying it on a laptop or computer screen. This is useful for web designers who want to show their clients their design and how it would look on a computer.

5. **App Mockup** – Google 'free app mockup templates'.

6. **CD/Album Cover Mockup** – Once again, Google 'free CD/Album cover mockup templates'.

7. **Logo Design** - You don't have to be a graphic designer or even own any graphic design software to create logos. Use a free website like LogoYes or Shopify free logo creator to make the logos.

8. **App Icon** - There are a lot of ways you can go about creating one, including generators online, but the best way is to find a template and use it.

9. **FB Timeline Cover Photos** - There are a lot of free tools you can use to generate a great looking timeline photo. Cover Junction, Timeline Cover Banner, Pic Scatter, and FaceitPages will all do the job.

10. **Ad Banners** - Look for free templates online that are the most common dimensions for ads and use those to create simple ads for your buyers.

11. **Favicons** - You can create one from scratch or ask your buyer to send you a logo/image that you will then convert to a favicon for them with a free converter.

12. **Photo Touch-up/Red Eye Removal** – There are plenty of free online tools and iPhone apps that allow you to do this.

13. **Simpsons/South Park Character** - Using this Simpsons character creator or this South Park character creator, you can complete an order in 10 minutes.

14. **Edit Photos/Graphics** - Simple graphic design jobs like saving images in different formats, changing the colour of objects, and deleting the background from images are all quick jobs you could charge $5 for on Fiverr.

15. **Turn Photos into Digital Paintings** - Quickly and easily turn someone's photo into a digital painting with either Photoshop (lots of tutorials online) or with a free tool.

Writing

16. **Write/Spin Articles** - You can choose to either write the articles from scratch (recommend 100 words per $5) or spin them with Spinbot (recommend 500 words per $5). Spinning essentially involves finding an article from a site like EzineArticles.com related to the niche your buyer wants, then using a spinner or rewriter like WordAi to rewrite the article for you so it passes all plagiarism checkers and duplicate content checkers.

17. **Edit Articles** - If you have the patience to proofread and edit people's work, you can use advanced editing software like Grammarly to edit 1000 words in 10 minutes.

18. **Book Reviews** - Offer a verified review (a review where you purchase their book and then review it) and in your gig extras, allow buyers to cover the cost of their book if it's not free.

19. **App Reviews** - App reviews are big on Fiverr, especially for the Android. If you have an iPhone but not an Android device, I would recommend downloading the Android emulator BlueStacks to leave Android app reviews. Remember to include gig extras or encourage multiples to cover the cost of paid apps.

20. **Listing/Directory Reviews** - A lot of businesses have listings on sites like TripAdvisor, Google Places, and Foursquare with no reviews and often times to come to Fiverr looking for someone to leave a review.

21. **Press Release Writing/Press Release Submission** - Google 'Press release template' and use that for this kind of gig. You could also submit the buyer's press release as a gig extra or a separate gig altogether. Here's a good list of sites to distribute to that are free.

22. **Write Sales Copy/Headlines/Taglines** – You can copy write for businesses.

23. **Comments on Blogs/Videos/Social Media** - Leave comments on people's blogs, YouTube videos or even Instagram photos. Works better if you use multiple accounts and use proxies so you don't get blocked. Just type in 'free proxies' on Google then run them through a free proxy checker to see which ones are fresh and working.

24. **Indiegogo Campaign** - Contribute $1 to Fiverr user's Indiegogo campaigns, share campaign on Facebook and leave a comment for $5 on Fiverr.

25. **Transcribe Audio/Video** - Transcribe 30 seconds of audio for $5. This is a great gig that can make you a nice hourly rate, especially if you're a good typer.

26. **Write 'About Us' Pages** - There are a lot of templates you if you search on Google for 'About us templates' that you can use to write up great About Us pages for company websites that require it.

27. **Write 'Terms and Conditions' and 'Privacy Policy'** - Search for Terms and Conditions or Privacy Policies 'generator' or 'template'.

28. **Write Resume or Cover Letter** - Ask your buyer what kind of job they are applying for and ask for their work experience and education and insert that into a resume or cover letter template for the kind of job or industry they're applying for.

29. **Critique Resume** - You don't have to be a job expert or a recruiter, you can quickly critique a 1 or 2-page resume for $5.

30. **Translation Services** - If you are a bi-lingual this is a great in-demand gig. You could even use a free translator and correct the translation so that it is correct. I would recommend 50 words for $5.

31. **Article Submission** - You can manually submit articles as either a gig extra or separate gig for your buyers.

SEO (Search Engine Optimisation)

32. **Keyword Analysis** - Use a keyword analysis tool like Ultimate Niche Finder to create excel reports for buyers showing keyword competition. You can also use Google's Keyword Planner tool.

33. **Domain Research** - Create a gig where you will do domain research for a company and create a report showing which domains are available for their brand/niche that would work best. I like to use Who.Is.

34. **Niche Research** - Perform niche research or supply buyers with a niche that has a good average monthly search on Google and a high CPM for advertisers, meaning it's a great

    niche to build a website for and place AdSense ads on. Ultimate Niche Finder is a great tool for this.

35. **Backlinks** - Find backlink packages for $1 on SEO Clerks and resell them on Fiverr for $5 (we will get into more detail on this in the outsourcing section).

36. **Send Traffic to Website** - Find traffic services for $1 on SEO Clerks and resell them on Fiverr for $5.

37. **Submit Businesses to Listings -**A lot of small and local businesses don't have listings on websites like Yellow Pages and Google Places. Create them for them for $5.

Social Media

38. **Tweet Messages to Followers** - If you have a lot of Twitter followers or create an account and buy a lot of Twitter followers for it, you can sell Twitter messages/ads to your followers for $5.

39. **Social Signals** - Buy social signals to a website such as Facebook shares and Google pluses from SEO Clerks and resell them on Fiverr for $5.

40. **Twitter Followers** - Twitter followers are highly in-demand. There are a lot of $1 gigs on SEO Clerks that you can resell for $5 on Fiverr.

41. **Facebook Likes** - Resell Facebook page and post likes on Fiverr from SEO Clerks.

42. **YouTube Views/Likes/Subs** - SEO Clerks is a great place to resell YouTube services from.

43. **Instagram Likes/Followers** - Instagram is very much in-demand, especially Instagram likes. Resell $1 SEO Clerks Instagram gigs for $5 on Fiverr.

44. **Pinterest Followers/Repins** - SEO Clerks is a great place to resell from on Fiverr, once again, we will get into more detail on this in the following section.

45. **Create Facebook Fanpage/Page for Business** - Many business owners don't know how to even create a Facebook page for their own business.

46. **Setup Social Media, Create YouTube Channel** - You can have a package where you create pages on all major media services for the buyer's small business on sites like YouTube and Twitter either as a gig extra or separate gig.

47. **Manage Social Media** - Create a gig where you will manage a company's website for a day.

48. **Share Links/Promos to Twitter/Facebook** - Share a link to a company website to all your Facebook friends and all your social media profiles.

49. **Create and Sell Accounts** - You can create accounts for social media websites and sell them on Fiverr. You may need to use proxies and create email addresses for each account. You may need to phone verify accounts as well.

Video
___

50. **Video Testimonials/Spokesperson/Review** – Get a good camera/smartphone and act as a reviewer/spokesperson.

51. **Product Testimonials** - Ask for your buyer to mail you a physical product, or record yourself using a virtual one, such as an app, website or game. The idea is to record yourself using the product while providing a testimonial.

52. **5-Minute Video Critiques** – Record yourself critiquing for something like a website, product or app.

53. **Whiteboard Animations** - Go to Sparkol, sign up for a trial and learn the software in only minutes. It's very easy to use and great for creating brilliant animations. I would recommend $5 for 10 seconds of animation.

54. **Edit Video/Add Music/Graphics** - If you have Windows Movie Maker, you could do easy video edits for $5 such as adding music to videos, adding a watermark, etc.

55. **Convert Audio/Video Files to Other Formats** - There are many free converters you can use. For example, you can convert a YouTube video into an MP3 file.

Outsourcing

"For everything we don't like to do, there's someone out there who's really good, wants to do it and will enjoy it." – Josh Kaufman

Here is a method using Fiverr and SEOClerks. What we're going to do is visit SEOClerks, find something hot and re-sell it on Fiverr for profit. Fiverr takes 20% from each of your sales, hence cutting down profit per gig. You will need an investment of around $10 for this method. So, let's get started.

Psychologically, users of Fiverr are used to seeing $5 per gig (or £3.98 if you are in the UK). No matter what the value of the gig, sellers will sell if for $5 or the multiple of $5 (or its equivalent in the country you are in). So, in the mind of buyers, when they see an offer, they know $5 is low as it goes. This is where SEOClerks comes in handy.

SEOClerk is a marketplace similar to Fiverr, but with less popularity and doesn't fix the price at $5. Something you would like to resell. As you can see, there are hundreds of gigs at the price of only $1. You would have to put that same service (tweaking the headline and description, making it stand out) on Fiverr for $5. Giving you $3 profit after you pay the user on SEOClerks and Fiverr's commission.

Always put your delivery time on Fiverr one day longer than the delivery time listed on SEOClerk. That way, you will have time to receive the completion message from SEOClerk, then paste it to respond to the fiverr buyer. You can also either add your own tags or copy them and tweak it.

Another similar method to this is one you can use with UpWork and Fiverr.

What you want to do is find something on UpWork that you want to do. Head over to UpWork and go to 'find jobs' and type something in that you want to outsource. Let's outsource someone's logo for this example.

Let's take the first listing.

Sort by: Newest

Logo, branding and graphic designer

Fixed-Price - Expert ($$$) - Est. Budget: $250 - Posted 10 hours ago

5 designs choice from , PSD , EPS , Ai format custom made / branding book + style guide for each of the following Snappy America, Motor Club USA, Snappy America with Motor Club USA being the highlight, and Motor Club USA with Snappy America being the ... more

Skills: Logo Design   Graphic Design

As you can see the budget of the user is $250. What you want to do next is head over to Fiverr and search for someone that can complete what the person on UpWork requested. Look for someone reputable on Fiverr that can complete this job.

As you can see, the markup here is insane, merely $5 can make you $250. Many large agencies make money using these exact methods. They may charge $1000 for a nice logo, and they will outsource the work to UpWork for it to be completed for $20.

Another example of this would be cold calling businesses telling them you boost their Google ranking (or anything else). And once they agree, you can outsource the work. However, I will get into greater detail on how to start your own agency later. Hence why I believe selling is the single most important skill you can have in regards to making money.

Social Media

"Good salespeople sell value and social media is the best place to find this value because of its transparency." – Gary Vaynerchuk

As mentioned in my introduction, I will not be covering anything you can find in a quick Google search. So, if you need help setting up and how to grow them, Google it. Instead, I will be teaching what only people within the social scene know that they do not want others to know, which isn't readily available everywhere online.

Deciding What You Want to Do

You must ask yourself what path you want to go down and the purpose of your social media account.

You have 3 primary options:

- Creating a personal brand.
- Creating a niche account with a high following/engagement.
- Using it to promote your business.

The Platforms

Twitter

Twitter remains as one of the most used social media platforms, the short message communication tools allows you to post tweets up to 140 characters long. Twitter is a great place to interact and connect with your audience.

Instagram

This is undoubtedly one of the best social media channels; I suggest everyone should be on it. Instagram allows you to put visual content in front of your target audience. This is arguably the best platform for connecting with influencers on. You can also link all your other social accounts such as Facebook and Twitter to your account, within the settings.

Facebook

The biggest social networking platform, currently seeing an increase in traffic with older people along with the young. This remains a dominant platform for both organic and paid reach. I highly suggest you spend hours learning how to execute Facebook Ads well (along with Instagram Ads, since I will not be going into this).

Snapchat

A quick emerging platform that allows for 10-second video clips and pictures, has a huge user base with more than 150 million daily users. This platform is very popular amongst younger people but is slowly increasing in popularity with adults. This is a great platform to create a very loyal customer base that you can update daily, great for showing behind the scenes.

Youtube

Youtube allows for videos of any length to be posted and viewed it is a great long form of media. This is a great platform since you can monetize this platform from direct Ads along with being paid as an influencer (like all other platforms).

Ways to Monetize

I will not be covering how to grow your account because there are hundreds of useful practical guides on how to do that, so look into that first since you will need a good following before you should monetize. Just remain patient – every social media account once had zero followers.

The primary methods of monetizing social media are:
- Sponsoring a Product or Service / Sell Shoutouts
- Affiliate Marketing
- Cost Per Action / Payment Per Install / Payment Per Download
- Promoting Your Product or Service
- Raise Awareness for Your Business
- Monetize Youtube Through Youtube Partnership / Amazon Affiliate
- Sell Your Account

Sponsoring Products

Getting paid as an influencer through sponsorships is simple enough, once you manage to grow a loyal following, businesses will start to contact you saying they will pay you in return for a shoutout (normally with their own discount code so owners can track sales), acting as the modern age of "celebrity endorsement". For example, if I were selling a new protein powder targeted at men, I would search Instagram and Youtube for a male influencer in the fitness industry that would fit my niche.

| 2,162 posts | 3.2 M followers | 58 following |

Contact · **Follow** · ▼

Ulissesworld ✓
Athlete
TURN ON MY POSTS NOTIFICATIONS ↗
◆ U Apparel Owner
◆ BiotechUSA
◆ Dedication Has No Limitations.
◆ Bookings | Ulisses@jagchima.com

I found this user for my example; most influencers will leave their email or Kik in their bio so that you can contact them regarding business opportunities and such. A great example of someone successfully sponsoring products would be the Youtuber 'Alpha M', I suggest you look at some of his videos and how he successfully integrates other's products and gets huge amounts of money for it.

If you can successfully build an audience, whether you only have 2000 followers who actively engage with you or 20 million. You can use your social media presence for sponsorships or even shoutouts. The price of a 24-hour shoutout for an account with 5-10% engagement per 100k follower's costs around $50 at the time of writing (but this also depends on the niche).

| 1,025 posts | 2.2 M followers | 603 following |

Contact · **Follow** · ▼

Millionaire Mentor ✓
Organization
· #1 Entrepreneur Lifestyle Publication

An account like this would charge around $1000 per shoutout. As you can obviously tell, if an account like this gives two shoutouts like this a day, they would be making thousands every day, not to mention the other ways the account is monetizing their account. Let's take an example of a shoutout they might give.

MAKE A CUSTOMER, NOT A SALE."

@JULESMARCOUX

♥ 13,241 likes

millionaire_mentor Great quote from @julesmarcoux - it's all about playing the long term game and creating customers. Make sure you follow him 👉 @julesmarcoux

View all 69 comments

Jules will have paid hundreds, if not thousands for this shoutout, in order to grow his audience. When you have an active audience, others will approach you for sponsorships and shoutouts (both on your platform, Twitter, on forums and Flipmass).

You can use your social media presence as a platform for either your own product (e.g. eCommerce store or a program) or someone else's (whether you get paid directly or through an affiliate marketing scheme).

Affiliate Marketing

Affiliate marketing is when you promote another product or service and gain a commission for every sale. Since affiliate marketing is so popular, there are hundreds of free resources and different methods you can find online to help you. For my example, I will be showing you how you could monetize your blog through affiliate marketing with Amazon affiliates.

Firstly, you will want to provide value to your audience in your niche and then provide something of value to them that they could purchase. Let's take my blog as an example. I will write a summary for a book.

Doing The Impossible - Book Summary

The 25 Laws of Doing The Impossible:

Recreate Yourself

Law 1 - Invest in Your Identity

Law 2 - Let The Right Ones In

Law 3 - Protect Your Credibility Score

Law 4 - Strengthen Your Greatest Weapon

Law 5 - Challenge Your Way of Thinking

Law 6 - Know Your Why

Law 7 - Work Like It's 1880

Law 8 - Elevate Imagination To a Whole New Level

Law 9 - Be as Curious as Alice

Law 10 - Break Away from the Old You

"The standard Amazon affiliate link gives you 24 hours for a customer to make a purchase, in order for you to earn a commission.

This means that if a customer clicks your link and orders anything (almost anything), within a 24-hour window, you'll earn a commission on those items. It's a universal cookie, meaning that even if the customer clicks through your link to view a baby stroller, but ends up buying a new kitchen set, some dumbbells, and a ribbon for their dog, you'll get paid for all of those items. As soon as the customer places an order, your cookie is wiped. Even if they come back 1 hour later and order more things, you won't get paid."

At the end of the blog, I will leave the link to the book via my amazon affiliate link and whoever clicks on and purchases anything on amazon in the next 24 hours, I will get up to a 10% commission. So, I would search amazon for the link to the book like so:

I would then get the link to the book with my affiliate link and paste it into a code block on my blog.

As always, thanks for reading this short book summary, if you would like it in more detail, I suggest you pick up the book, it is an extremely good read.

Book Link - Doing The Impossible

You can do this with any type of product, whether you want to do make-up video's on youtube and link the products used in the description. Or you want to look for another affiliate marketing site that allows a higher commission of around 40-50% with specific people or websites such as jvzoo.com or ClickBank. Nevertheless, I suggest you provide the value first and therefore you are a credible source and have leverage. A cold sale online is very difficult.

Cost Per Action

CPA, which stands for Cost per Action, is a form of affiliate advertisement that is used by almost all companies throughout the world to generate leads for their products. This marketing is done by affiliates who work through their own websites to send traffic to the advertiser's website for the product of the company. CPA deals with specific forms of marketing which involve pay per click and pay per lead ads.

The great thing about CPA networking is that you get paid even if you don't manage to sell the product that your company is making. If the individual, who visits your website clicks on an advertisement, downloads a newsletter, signs up for a regular subscription or simply goes ahead and buys the product, you get paid in commission. This can range on the low side from 50 pence to £50.

CPA marketing plans to gain useful information from potential consumers and convert them into profitable leads for future sales generation. This information can be of various kinds: telephone number, residential address, email address, social security number, credit or debit card number, etc.

I'm not going into any more detail on CPA since there are hundreds of free resources that can teach you this step by step.

Promoting Your Product or Service

You can use a large social media following in conjunction with a Shopify store where you can sell anything from apparel to same niche products (see eCommerce section on how to do this). You can also create a program or service (see program and eBook section).

Let's take a fitness social media influencer and see what they could sell:

- A product such as protein shakes/gym gear.
- A program / eBook on how to lose weight (give away at least 90% of your content away for free).
- Sell private one to one coaching / personal training.

Here is an example of someone who monetizes successfully:

| | 1,554 posts | | 115 k followers | | 1,642 following |

Contact   **Follow**

Brandon Carter
Public Figure
Failed Musician
Best Selling Author of 5 books
Over 80 Mill YouTube views.
Over 1.5 Million Facebook fans
Snapchat - KillerCarter187
BicepBible.com/
New York, New York

He provides a lot of free content but also monetizes with books, programs and his own supplement line. The reason why you should always give back to your audience for free is due to the liking and authority bias, we are more likely to buy from those who we see as experts and that we like. Look at the top people within your niche and you will learn a lot.

Flipping Accounts on Social Media

Another method to make money on social media is through buying and selling accounts.

Let's take an account I managed to grow from scratch and see how much it is listed for on Flipmass (an app where influencers buy and sell accounts and shoutouts).

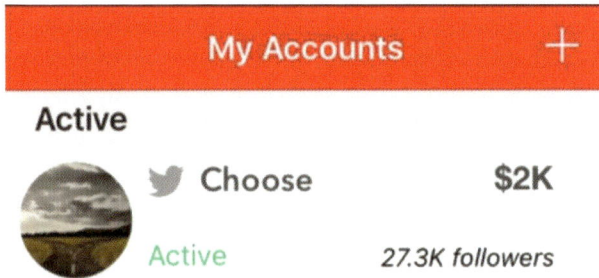

If you do not wish to directly monetize the account, people are always buying accounts, and this is how you can make money. To give you an idea as to what some of the biggest social media accounts are worth, below is an image of the accounts selling at the highest prices, and some other prices of smaller accounts.

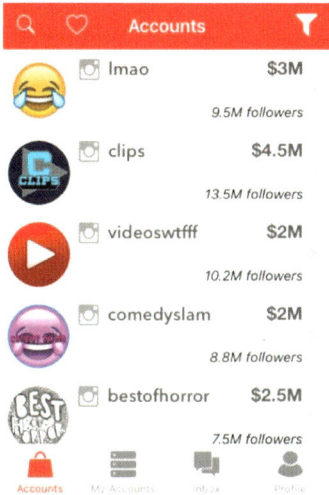

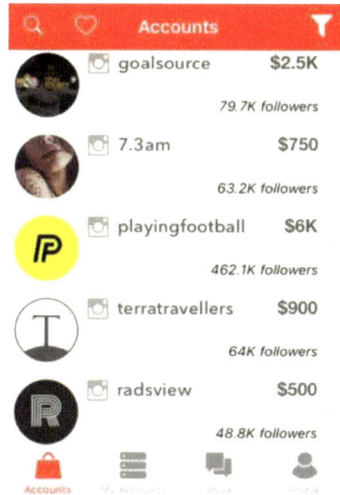

Flipping Accounts Using Forums / Flipmass

Before you follow through with the method I am about to share with you, you must spend time in the social media scene to understand the pricing, supply and demand of accounts so you do not take a loss, since this can be very high risk.

For this method, you will need an investment of anywhere between £100-10000 first.

This is what you should do:
1. First is create a personal twitter account on twitter.
2. You will need to DM @Flipmass after you sign up and download their app requesting a code (you must provide them proof of your identity).
3. Your next step is to browse / post a thread on a forum that allows for the selling of social media accounts such as OGFlip or Forum Korner stating you're looking for STAT accounts (an account with a high number of followers) on Twitter/Instagram/Snapchat. After a while of being in the

      social media game, you will be able to tell how much accounts are worth. If you do not know, please contact me.

4. Now whenever you find a STAT with an organic audience worth $500 you can list it on Flipmass with a price higher than the sellers asking price.

Now, you may be thinking, what? You can't make good money with this.

But, you're wrong, there are two prices in the social media market, the one on forums, and the one on twitter and between influencers who do this for a living rather than a side hustle as influencers have more money to throw around. This means that you can purchase STAT accounts much cheaper on forums such as HF and sell for much more on Flipmass (note that Flipmass takes a 5% fee).

You can easily negotiate on forums and mark up your price on Flipmass by 2-5x more. E.g. you see someone is selling a Snapchat STAT for $500,

Look at other accounts on Flipmass and list it around the same price, you will see that Flipmass prices are 2-3x higher if not more (in most cases). If you know the market, this will make you money. I will show you an example of how this worked for me:

I purchased an OG Snapchat STAT for $220.

■■■■■■■ Wrote:
Can you middleman the snapchat neymar for $220 BTC with the user ■■■ please bro?

Yeah add my skype: ■■■■

Stories

My Story
Tue 19:47

Tue 19:47   21.3K 👁
                                                    199 ✈

Tue 04:35   31.6K 👁
                                                     11 ✈

Tue 03:53   32.5K 👁
                                                     84 ✈

As you can see, the seller of the account was not aware of the real value of the account. After I purchased the account, I ended up selling 10 shoutouts for $50 each ($500 total) before I decided I want to sell it on Flipmass. I agreed I will not share how much I sold the account for, however, here are some other accounts that might allow you to guess roughly how much I sold the account on for, considering mine was OG and had a very good niche.

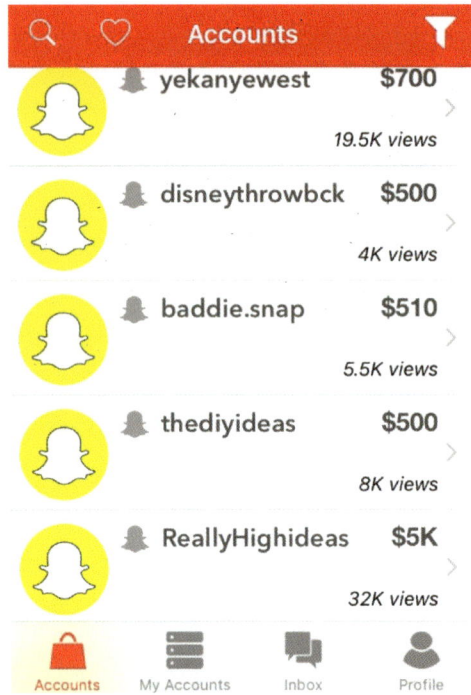

Tips:

- You can purchase followers for $1/k which will drive the prices up if you want to purchase the account before listing it.
- An OG username will drive up the price (if you own the account).
- If you do not want to risk it, you can always list before purchasing and then buy the account off the user on your forum after you get an offer on Flipmass. However, you are not allowed to list accounts you do not own (so be prepared, and don't post huge accounts as they will probably be known within the community).
- Be cautious. Make sure you know the market – do not run into this straight away. Also, always remember to use a trusted middleman and request the OG email and secure the account fully, to ensure the user does not pull the account back.

Email Marketing

"Signing up is a powerful signal of intent to buy. Send them valuable emails until they do." –
Jordie van Rijn

Introduction

In this section, I will teach you how to create and grow an email list which you can monetize. Email marketing is one of the most scalable businesses that can make you millions yearly if you execute the Ads well. This is a (HIS) high scalable business, rather than a (CF) cash flow business, which does not require a lot of money. With a list of just 10000, you would make around £100,000 every year.

The target of this is to create an opt-in web page for our niche and provide something of value for free so that people enter their email address to receive it. After they add their email, you will market valuable products to them, whether it be yours, or through affiliate marketing.

Building Your Opt-In Page

Your first step is to create your opt-in page. If you do not know how to code it from scratch, I suggest using Lead Pages; it has a list of templates which you can edit until you are happy. Let's build one together, the simpler the opt-in page, the better it will convert. I am going to choose the Super Basic Squeeze.

DRAG & DROP TEMPLATE
Simple Report Squeeze Page
FREE

DRAG & DROP TEMPLATE
Super Basic Squeeze Page
FREE

DRAG & DROP TEMPLATE
Webinar Thank You Page
FREE

DRAG & DROP TEMPLATE
Basic Centered Squeeze Page
FREE

After some editing and choosing a niche for helping eCommerce owners, I ended up with the following landing page.

100% **FREE** CHEAT LIST PDF DOWNLOAD

101 OF THE MOST PROFITABLE SHOPIFY NICHES WITH SUPER LOW COMPETITION IN 2017

EACH OF THESE NICHES CAN GENERATE OVER $1000+ EVERY DAY!

0	11	26	42
DAYS	HOURS	MINUTES	SECONDS

REMAINING UNTIL THIS IS REMOVED

GET INSTANT ACCESS

Your Information is 100% Secure And Will Never Be Shared With Anyone!

© 2017 - Neema Imantabari | Legal Information

Let me run you through what makes this a very high converting webpage:
- Stressing how it is 100% free, and quickly says what it is.
- Shows how the user gets the niches.
- Specificity - shows detail and authority.
- Handles doubts someone may have, e.g. shows the niches are very profitable.
- Adds time constraint, adds urgency through the countdown.

- Instant gratification 'Get Instant Access.'
- Adds more trust through 'legal information' and 'your information is 100% secure and will never be shared with anyone.'
- Clear call to action. ✳
- You could add social proof to show how other people use it.
- Run split tests (AB testing) to see what type of landing page converts the best.

×

ALMOST THERE! PLEASE COMPLETE THIS FORM TO GAIN INSTANT ACCESS

Enter Your Email Address to Immediately Get The 101 Best Shopify Niches

E-mail

Neema@Neemalmantabari.com

GET MY NICHES NOW

Privacy Policy: We hate SPAM and promise to keep your email address safe

Creating Your Autoresponder

An autoresponder is used to hold your list of customers and also allows us to automatically mass message them.

I use my own personal autoresponder when email marketing. However, to help you, I will be using a web-based mailer, Aweber for this example. There are other autoresponders you can use, such as GetResponse, MailChimp, Drip or Market Hero.

First, you will want to register for AWeber's free trial and fill out the necessary information. I suggest you head over to settings and then confirmed opt-in. And turn off the send confirmation for opt-in emails for web forms, since at this point all we want is people to get onto the email list.

Send a confirmed opt-in email for Web Forms:

off

Send a confirmed opt-in email for Imports:

off

What we are going to do next is create the sign-up form and link it to lead pages. Click on the sign-up form shown on the page. After which, you will be met with a page that will look like this:

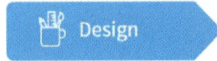

If you want to, you can make the form look nice, however, for my example, I am just showing you how it works. Then head over to the settings where you will need to fill out the following to a page you will create on Lead Pages.

Basic Settings Customize your forms properties.

Form Name*:

Test For Book

Thank You Page:

| Custom Page | ▾ | [**Preview**]

http://imantabari.com/thanks

☑ Open this in a new window

Already Subscribed Page:

| Custom Page | ▾ |

http://imantabari.com/thanks

⚙ Hide Advanced Settings

Next, save and publish your form and click on 'I will install my form' and copy the code.

Who Will Publish This Form To Your Website?

I Will Install My Form
You are comfortable with HTML and have access to edit your pages

| **Javascript Snippet** The Quick and Easy Version | Raw HTML Version Advanced Design Customization |

Recommended

- If you change your form here, you won't have to update your website.
- Track statistics in your account.

You can paste the snippet below anywhere between the body tags of your website:

```
<div class="AW-Form-2072116245"></div>
<script type="text/javascript">(function(d, s, id) {
  var js, fjs = d.getElementsByTagName(s)[0];
  if (d.getElementById(id)) return;
  js = d.createElement(s); js.id = id;
  js.src = "//forms.aweber.com/form/45/2072116245.js";
```

Then head back over to Lead Pages where your final confirmation for the email is (for me it is after I press, 'Get Instant Access').
A new page will load where people fill their details out. When there, create an HTML code box and paste the code.

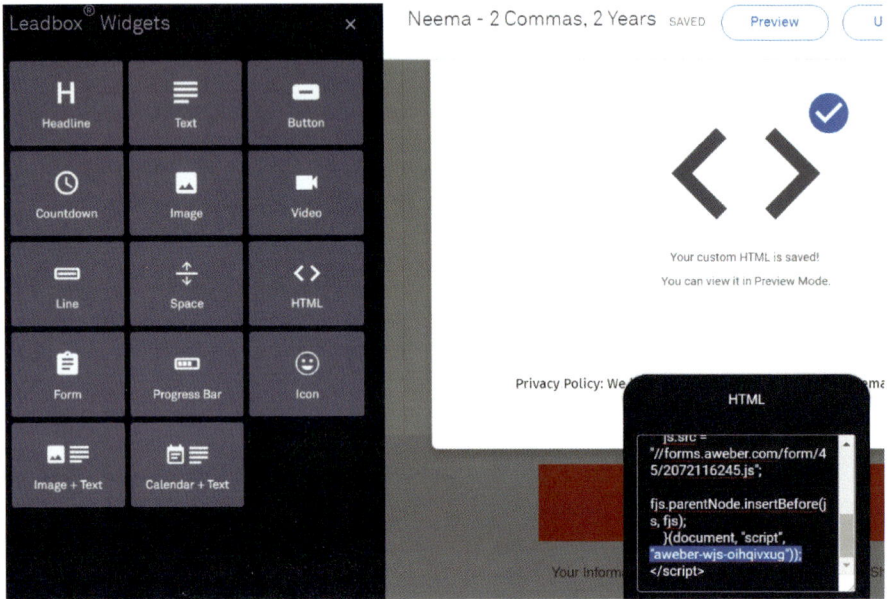

I also suggest while on Lead Pages you go to integrations under settings and link your Aweber account to your Lead Pages account.

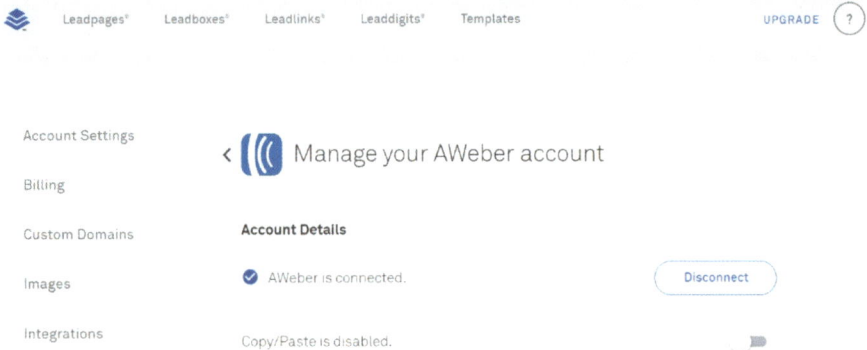

After completing these steps, go to preview and test if filling out the form works.

Enter Your Email Address to Immediately Get The 101 Best Shopify Niches

Name: Book Test

Email: BookTest2C2Y@gmail.com

Get My Niches Now

As you can see, it does not look the nicest or the most professional, but if you put time into it, it will look beautiful and convert extremely well.

After someone completes their details, they will be redirected to the URL you entered on Aweber and their information will be saved on Aweber for future marketing.

☐   ‣ Book Test   booktest2c2y@gmail.com   **Subscribed** Today, 3:05pm

Your next step is to go on Aweber, messages and to campaigns.

New Campaign

Give your campaign a name:

Follow Up

Don't worry you can always change this later

Create   Cancel

You can now create a campaign to follow up emails and schedule them to your liking.

Start Campaign: On Subscribe	⇄ **Replace Trigger**
Trigger campaign for **All subscribers**	
✉ Send Message:	
🕐 Wait: **5 days** before performing the next action	
✉ Send Message:	
🕐 Wait: **2 days** before performing the next action	
✉ Send Message:	

You can use their custom drag and drop email sender to schedule emails. This is the funnel I suggest you follow:

1. Opt-in.
2. Welcome email.
3. Value email.
4. Value email.
5. Small product pitch.
6. Value email.
7. Value email.
8. Small product pitch.
9. Value email.
10. Big pitch.

That is the funnel I suggest you for you. For every two/three value emails, one pitch is acceptable.

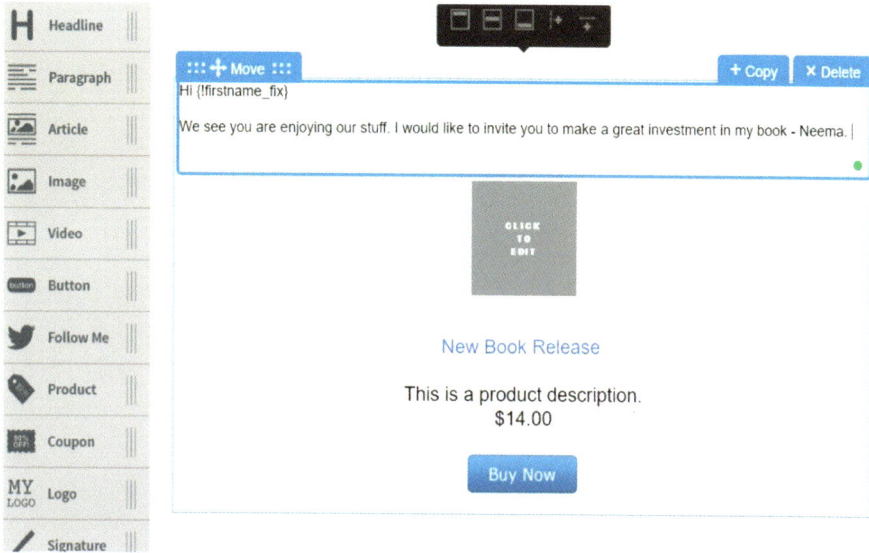

You are now done with setting everything up, let's get into how to get traffic and how to monetize your email lists. Remember to write and link your pdf file, depending on your niche.

How to Build Email Lists & Drive Traffic

Free Traffic

By posting good valuable content, you will grow through word of mouth and will be able to build trust and rapport with your audience.

A great place which you can use to drive free traffic to your opt-in page is social media. I am going to focus on Instagram and how you can use it get customers.

Firstly, you want to create an Instagram account around your niche. Please use Google to learn how you can grow a following on social media.

Here is a basic overview you will want to follow for free traffic:

1. Find other people within your niche by going to the biggest accounts on your niche and following all the followers of that account (software such as InstaEasy/Instagress or SlackSocial for FB can automate this whole process that I am about to share). What will then happen is once you follow these people and the bigger accounts is people will start to follow you back who are interested in your content.
2. Post quality content on your page and have your opt-in page in your account bio. I have found for every 10 posts; it is optimal to go for a direct post saying 'Click the link in my bio for 101 of the best shopify niches'. You do not want to spam your audience too much. "Give, give, give and then ask" – Gary Vaynerchuk.

Another great platform you can do this is on Twitter. You can automate follows with are free Google extensions such as Twitter follower or tweepi. This allows you to follow the followers of bigger accounts, without doing it manually. You can even head over to the search bar on Twitter and type in the problem that the pdf in your opt-in page solves. For example, I would search "Best Shopify Niches?" and custom messages people needing help by linking them to my opt-in page. I do not suggest using spammy methods such as crowdfire, to automatically direct message, anyone that follows you with your opt-in page link, instead focus on adding value. You can use these ideas on any platform, whether you are finding similar niche videos on youtube and posting links in the comments or posting them in Facebook groups.

Excluding social media, forums are also a great place to build email lists. For example, for my niche of Shopify niches that I choose, a forum based around internet marketing such as warrior forums would be great. The majority of forums have a free giveaway section, where you can provide your opt-in page directly on the thread or through private messages (check the forum rules if you are allowed to do this). This is a win-win situation, you get a free email, and they get what they wanted.

This is a great representation on how your content marketing should work.

Content Marketing Sales Funnel

The only problem with free marketing methods are that it can be very time-consuming, therefore, if you have some money you want to experiment with, I would suggest running paid Ads, which we will get into in the next section.

Paid Traffic

As the name suggests, this is traffic that you pay for, why I recommend you use paid traffic is that you can grow much quicker. I do not recommend buying lists of emails and spamming them, since you will end up just getting banned and your conversions will be incredibly low, along with the fact that using databases / using 3rd parties to get other's emails is unethical.

An example of paid Ads is Google AdWords, which can get you the top spot in Google without putting time into SEO. The downside to AdWords is that the cost per click (CPC) is very high, especially if you're covering a popular topic. And setup and management can be quite time-consuming.

Facebook ads, on the other hand, is quite easy to set up, and the CPC is usually much lower. With Facebook Ads, you can get in front of people who expressed an interest in your topic, without putting time into building a social media following. For this reason, I highly suggest you use FB Ads to promote your opt-in page. You can create test Ads for as low as $5, meaning there is little financial risk. When putting out your Ads, I highly suggest you post your Ads with a direct approach. For example, make your Ad say exactly what you are providing so people would not click on your Ad unless they know what they were about to get. Therefore, I recommend paying per click rather than impressions. This is because if you work out your cost per lead (CPL) and customer long-term value (CLV) you will be able to scale your business to the moon. It is simple math. Once you know it costs $3 per lead, but every lead generates $10 within the first one, all you will have to do is purchase Ads to scale this.

Bid amount	Automatic - Let Facebook set the bid that helps you get the most link clicks at the best price.
	• Manual - Enter a bid based on what link clicks are worth to you.
	$3.78 per link click
	Suggested bid: $2.19 USD ($1.73–$3.03)
When you are charged	Impression
	• Link Click (CPC)

Let's look at a great Facebook Ad I found online, within an SEO niche.

As you can see, nearly everyone who clicks on this link will opt-in since it is very clear what it is providing. It clearly states what it does and stipulates that very simply and quickly. You could even go as far as to host giveaways and promote them through Facebook or any other social media platform to get a huge audience.

Another excellent paid method is paying influencers within your niche for a shoutout. For example, if you have a list of the best Shopify niches, you might want to message big motivational / success accounts to give you shoutouts and put your opt-in page in their bio for a certain amount of time.

Monetize Your Email List

This section will be very similar to the social media section since monetizing is fundamentally the same, so I highly suggest you read that section first.

What you want to do once you start growing your list is going on your autoresponder and start promoting products, whether directly yours or through affiliate marketing by emailing your list.

You can head over to one of the following affiliate marketing sites to find suitable products to provide to your niche, if they purchase / or complete an action (depending on if it's CPA or affiliate marketing) after clicking on the link in your email, you gain a commission. Here are some affiliate marketing sites you may want to consider, I suggest you take a look for yourself as well.

- JVZoo
- ClickBank
- ShareASale
- OfferValut
- FlexOffers
- RevenueWire
- AvantLink
- LinkConnector
- Affiliate Window
- AffiliateNetwork
- AdMedia

There is so much free content to be found online, that I will not cover everything to do with affiliate marketing. You have all the resources to make thousands/millions in email marketing – best of luck!

2 Commas In 2 Years

eCommerce

"The reason it seems that price is all your customers care about is that you haven't given them anything else to care about." – *Seth Godin.*

In this section, I will be cover making money with eCommerce. We will be using Shopify to create your eCommerce store as it is the most beginner friendly.

If you are just starting out and don't have an existing store or product, your best bet is dropshipping. Dropshipping is a great way to begin an eCommerce business without stressing over stock or shipping. Instead of taking the risk of holding stock, you will purchase the product on Aliexpress once someone pays you on your store. You would then use your customer's shipping information when you are ordering on AliExpress.

AliExpress makes it simple to find items to sell on your store. The prices of everything on AliExpress are extremely low, allowing for high margins.

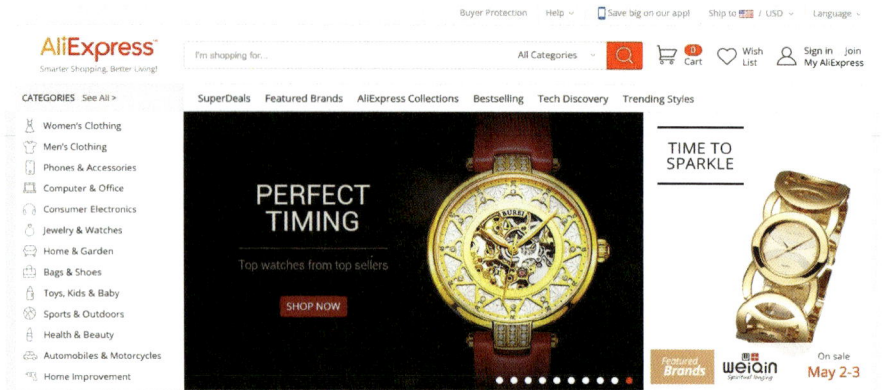

AliExpress is a huge marketplace with a wide selection of products you can sell in your store. As mentioned, since most of the AliExpress sellers are overseas manufacturers, their prices are very competitive.

All sellers on AliExpress understand that many their customers are resellers and are much more interested in dropshipping.

There's no upfront cost or fee, so you can test out products without any financial commitment. You can start dropshipping with AliExpress today for free.

Many sellers on AliExpress have great product photos that you can use on your website, as well as detailed product descriptions to help you describe the product in your store.

I will go over in more detail how this all comes together, what to look for in a product and seller, and how to position yourself for success, but it's not any more complicated than what I described above.

Now you may be wondering, why someone would someone buy from you when they can buy it for cheaper on AliExpress? With an AliExpress dropshipping business, your competitive advantage won't be your price or unique proprietary products. Your competitive advantage will be reaching your customers before competitors do and adding value to them through creating a nice brand, creating content and excellent customer service.

Setting Up Your Store

The first part of setting up your store is deciding on your niche. If you don't know where to start, begin with the product categories AliExpress has and see what interests you.

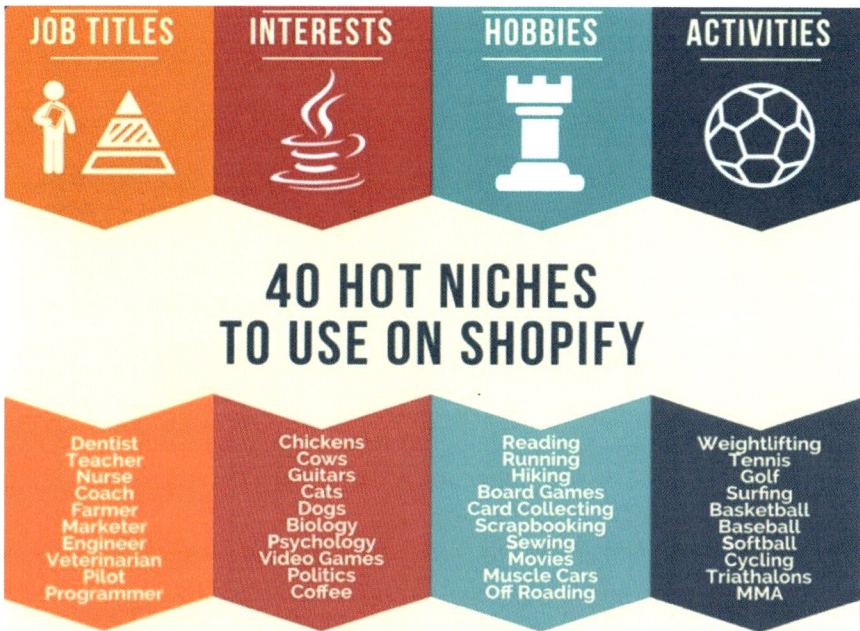

Once you have decided on a niche, it's time to start choosing products you want to resell on your store. In this example, I chose watches as my store niche.

As you'll find with AliExpress, there's a huge selection of products to choose from which can be overwhelming. Here are a few things I look for when selecting a product and supplier on AliExpress:

No Fakes and Brands - I suggest you avoid any brands to avoid reselling fakes and knockoffs. Look for unbranded products. If there's a logo on the product, I recommend avoiding it, even if it may be legitimate. This is because you are not a licensed reseller and because you don't actually know if the product is real.

Over 250 orders - A product with a lot of orders tells you a few things. First, it shows there's a demand for the product. Second, it tells you the supplier is reliable. Sometimes when looking for a new product, I'll sort products by the 'most orders' to see what products are the most popular that people buy.

Sort by: Best Match | Orders ▾ | Newest ▾ | Seller rating ▾ | Price ⬍

Over 4.5 stars rating - I also suggest the products you plan to resell has a high product rating (over 4.5 stars) and the seller has high positive feedback. I recommend you use the free Google Chrome extension called 'AliExpress Seller Check'. ⤳ *install*

Seller rating:

94.9% clients are happy with this seller

✅ It is more than 1 year in Aliexpress (**Since 2.07.2014**)

✅ High feedback rating of the seller

✅ More than 1000 sold goods, very high level of trust

✅ Majority of goods correspond to the description

✅ Communicative, well responds to messages

✅ Fast shipping

✅ Sold very high quantity of goods for the last 3 months

This provides you with a detailed overview rating left with a third-party app. This extension is a lot more reliable than only using AliExpress' rating system.

Low price with a high margin potential – Pick products with a low price which you can easily add value to.

Lots of great, unbranded, product photos - Do your due diligence to ensure the photos are actually from your manufacturer and not stolen from another retailer online. Doing a quick Google image search will help you see if the product photos are of a real brand and retailer or from the manufacturer themselves.

Communicative, helpful seller - Don't be afraid to ask a seller questions before placing an order with them. A good reliable seller will answer all of your questions quickly.

Creating Your Online Store

Now that you have your niche, you want to create your online store. There are so many free videos and articles on this if you would like to study it in even more detail, which I suggest, although this should cover almost everything.

You can start your Shopify store with a free, 14-day trial that you can sign-up for by simply Googling it. You will need to enter your email address, password and store name.

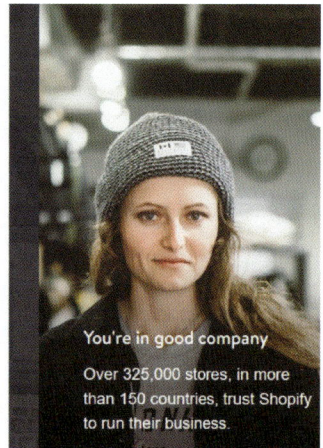

Start your free 14-day trial today!
No credit card required - no risk

Email address

Password

Your store name

Create your store

You're in good company
Over 325,000 stores, in more than 150 countries, trust Shopify to run their business.

Note that your store name will be included in your store's URL. Even though you can change this later, it's best to think of something simple. Here are the steps you will want to follow to create your store.

1 - Adding Products to Your Store

Your first step to creating your Shopify store is adding your products. This step is important to cover in detail because it's not as simple as copying the images and description of the AliExpress listing and placing that on your website. Instead, if you want to position your store for success, there are a few things you should consider:

Write your own product descriptions - The product descriptions for many of the products on AliExpress were not written by copywriters or with the intention of fully explaining the benefits of the products. Having your own unique content will serve your business better in the long run (Google ignores duplicate content) and will help you convert better on product pages.

Let customers know about delivery times - It's a good idea to include on your website that your customers may need to wait at least 30 days (depending on the vendor) for their order to arrive. Since most vendors on AliExpress are located in China, shipping times can be longer than average.

Use an order tracking app - With longer shipping times than most people are used to, you'll often receive emails from customers asking where their purchase is. Use an order tracking app from the Shopify App store to keep your customers up-to-date with the status of their purchase.

Offer free shipping - This can become one of your competitive advantages, so I highly recommend offering free shipping to your customers by taking advantage of the free/low-cost shipping provided by many AliExpress sellers. Or you can do the complete opposite and offer a free product and mark up the shipping costs (this is usually good for Facebook ads).

Price products appropriately - The truth is you are not starting out as Amazon, you will not be able to sell in huge volumes, so you will need to have a good margin to make it worthwhile. Another reason for this is that people do not buy what is incredibly cheap as they will see no value since it seems too good to be true. Instead of focusing on low prices, focus on creating so much value to your customers that price will not be an issue. When the value of your product/service exceeds the value of a customer's money, only then will they buy.

Add products to your store with apps – To speed up the process of adding products from AliExpress to your website, you can use either Oberlo or Expressfy to add products to your store quickly.

↳ Can do, but want to write own Product descriptions

2 - Customise your design

Next, you will want to add a custom design to your Shopify store by choosing a theme. The Shopify theme store has a great variety of designs to choose from free to paid and sorted by industry. I also suggest you get a logo for your store, you can get one made for $5 on fiverr.com.

→ or, make my own on Photoshop.

Explore free themes

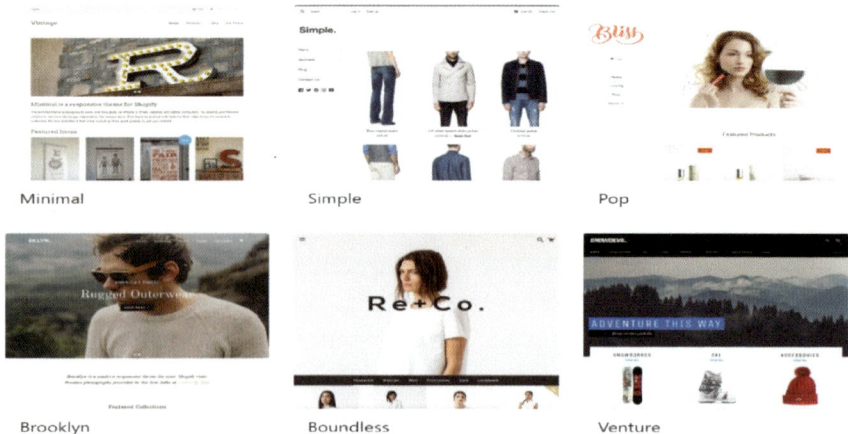

Minimal

Simple

Pop

Brooklyn

Boundless

Venture

Assuming you do not have the starter plan, you can edit your chosen theme by using the theme settings editor or template editor to modify the coding (HTML, CSS, and JS). You will want to go into the settings to modify the footer, as that is where you will add your social media links, payment methods, and other details such as privacy policies and refund guarantee stipulations.

3 – Set up your domain name

I highly suggest you invest in a domain for your store, instead of the.myshopify.com. You can purchase and set up your domain directly with shopify, or alternatively, you can connect it with a third party hoster such as namecheap.   GoDaddy

4 - Set up shipping and tax rates

You will need to choose to add additional shipping costs and taxes to your items or to let Shopify know you have included them in your item price. Shopify includes some basic rates to get you started, but depending on what you sell, you may need to customize more options.

5 - Set up payments

Perhaps the most important step after adding your products is setting up how customers will pay you. If you are in the UK, US or Canada you can accept payments with Shopify Payments that accept credit cards without needing to set up a third-pasty payment gateway or merchant account. Shopify also integrates with many different payments processing services including PayPal, Amazon Payments, BitPay and Google Wallet.

Your store accepts payments with Shopify Payments. View the <u>terms of service</u>.

Using: **Shopify Payments**　　　　　　　　　　　View Payouts　　Edit ▸

The safer, easier way to pay

6. Settings

You will want to go through your Shopify settings thoroughly. Most of these will be filled out while you complete the above steps, but a few things like the place where you add your Google Analytics code, store title, and store description are awaiting configuration in the general settings section.

7. Add Useful Applications

I suggest looking for good and useful apps, both for the aesthetics of your store and automation. Here are some of the applications I set up for my watch store.

	BEST Currency Converter	View details	🗑
	Bulk Discounts	View details	🗑
	Consistent Cart, Abandoned Cart Emails & More	View details	🗑
	Fraud Filter	View details	🗑
	Free Shipping Bar by Hextom	View details	🗑
	Plug in SEO	View details	🗑
	Quick Announcement Bar by Hextom	View details	🗑
	Quick View by Secomapp	View details	🗑
	Social Autopilot	View details	🗑
	TRUST	View details	🗑

8. Open your store to the world

Once you are ready, you can make your Shopify store public. Until you do, it will be password protected so you can do some testing to make sure things look and function the way they should. As with all things, be sure to do lots of testing so that customers aren't the first ones to find mistakes and glitches. Here is an example of a product I am selling on my store.

Below is a screenshot of the price of the product I am selling above on AliExpress.

Now your store is fully set up, you are ready to go, let's begin in acquiring your first customer and beyond.

How to Get Your First Sales

Send an Email to Your Pre-Launch List

If you have built a pre-launch list, then you're going to want to email this list before you do any other tactics. These people will likely be your most qualified leads when starting your online store since these people have already shown interest.

You can use a service like MailChimp or any one of the other great email apps. I recommend reading the email marketing section to best understand how you can build a list.

Run a Contest or Giveaway

Giveaways are a great way to get attention. Although it can be argued that giveaways mostly encourage interaction from people looking for a deal, if done correctly, the viral nature of a contest can garner a lot of initial traffic and word of mouth, expanding the presence and knowledge of your store and its products. Look on the Shopify app store to find great apps that can help enhance your giveaways.

Sell on eBay & Other Marketplaces

Being a successful entrepreneur requires testing everything, this includes testing other channels like marketplaces. Sites like eBay and Amazon can be great places to get some of your initial sales. These are ideal when starting because these marketplaces already have traffic and people searching for products. This provides you with a boost when first starting out, while you work on building your SEO and organic search results on Google.

Become Part of a Community

There are many forums you can join, simply type your niche followed by 'forums'. Reddit is a great forum, due to its sheer size. With thousands of subreddits, you're sure to find a community that has high levels of interest in your niche and product.

It's important to note that you can't just go in thinking you can sell your products in these communities. To make any community work for you, you must become part of the community and contribute. The payoff is not only potential sales to a highly-targeted group of people, but also a community of likeminded people you can create some great relationships. "Give, give, give and then ask." – Gary Vaynerchuk.

Launch Some Facebook Ads

Facebook allows for some of the most precise ad targeting features of any platform and is a channel all businesses should use. Keep in mind that although Facebook has some great targeting options, you really need to spend some time thinking about your target market, their lifestyle, the things they like and the things they don't like in order to find a good fit with your advertisements. When you first start

advertising on Facebook, you're likely going to pay a considerable amount for your first customers. Expect this, and spend some time tweaking your campaign and monitoring results.

Remember, your first sales shouldn't be about profitability. They should be about finding your product/market fit, and acquiring for your first customers to refine your advertising, shipping, fulfilment and customer service strategy, and experience. I suggest reading blog posts and watching videos from experts on Facebook Ads.

Utilise Instagram Paid Shoutout's

Instagram is a highly targeted visual marketing channel. Increasingly, brands are using influential account for sponsored product posts. The key here is to find large accounts (1,000-10,000,000 followers) and pay them to feature an image and caption of your choosing on their account.

Pricing ranges are based on the account and the engagement it receives. You can either directly message accounts regarding business, use Flipmass or social media forums.

Set up Google AdWords

Google AdWords is one of the most established advertising networks online. It's search based advertising so if you have a new product that no one has ever heard of before, you may want to consider skipping this.

The key to success with Google AdWords is constant monitoring and tweaking on your campaign. Just throwing a campaign up there isn't likely to be a winning strategy. Remember, just like Facebook Ads, your initial costs to acquire you first customer might be pricey, they may even exceed the total price of your product. But again, you goal should be to learn more about each channel and not necessarily profitability at the start. If your service is good, the customer will come back and purchase in the future so your CLV (customer lifetime value) will outweigh your CAC (customer acquisition cost).

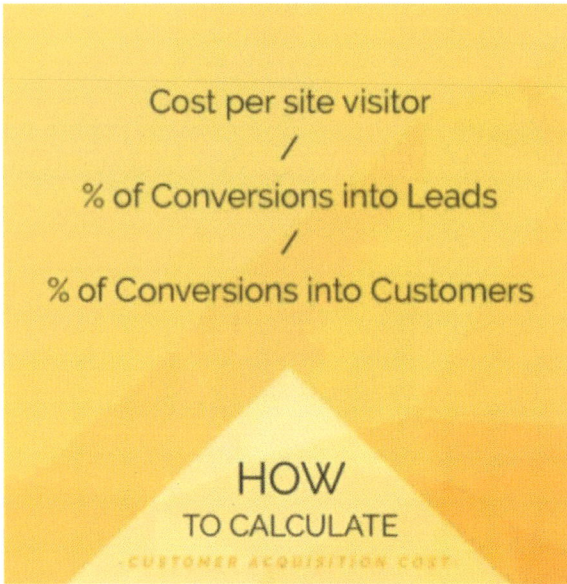

Cost per site visitor

/

% of Conversions into Leads

/

% of Conversions into Customers

HOW
TO CALCULATE
CUSTOMER ACQUISITION COST

Write an Outreach Blog Post

An outreach blog post is a post that usually highlights, quotes or features other influential people in your niche. These types of blog posts are a popular tactic to begin building relationships with influential people that matter in your niche and to (hopefully) get them to share your blog post with their audience.

To start, you'll want to make sure you craft a blog post with a purpose and that truly adds value. To do this, you'll want to write a blog post related to your product or niche and include links, quotes or profiles of influential people that are related to your niche.

Keep in mind that when quoting or linking to influencers, you'll want to start somewhat small, since you're still brand new. Look for influencers with blogs that have influence but aren't so big that your post and Tweets to them will go unnoticed.

Once you've written the post, you'll want to send a personal email to the people you highlighted in your post and let them know that you like their work and have included them in your most recent post. It's usually best not to ask for anything in return (to share it), rather, let them decide on their own regard. If the post was good, there's a good chance they will share it.

As an additional benefit, this blog post will start to become part of your SEO. The more you write, the more there is for Google to see, helping it rank you higher on Google.

Other Marketing Methods at a Glance

Social media

- Connect on Facebook
- Network on LinkedIn
- Provide Value on Youtube
- Spark Conversations on Twitter
- Inspire with Pinterest
- Work It on Instagram
- Create Content on Snapchat

Search Engine Optimisation

- Stand Out on Comparison Shopping Engines
- Get on Google Places
- Rank highly on other search engines. (e.g. Bing or Yahoo).
- Rank higher on Google (Using SEO)
- Learn from Web Analytics
- Be Accessible on Mobile Devices
- Get Product Reviews

- Write a Press Release
- Pull a PR Stunt
- Sell a Unique and Newsworthy Product
- Interview an Industry Influencer:

Content

- Write a Guest Post
- Create a Viral Video
- Write a Controversial Blog Post
- Create a YouTube Channel
- Build Your Email List

Paid Ads

- Advertise on Facebook
- Pay for Google AdWords
- Buy Banner Ads
- Promote Your Tweets on Twitter:
- Advertise on Instagram

Offline

- Get a Booth at a Flea Market or Farmer's Market
- Engage Your Local Business Network
- Say Hello to Strangers with Meetup.com
- Sell Wholesale to Other Retailers
- Take Your Business on the Road
- Deploy a Sales Team

Traditional Advertising

- Get Going with Tradeshows

- Go Door to Door
- Use Print Ads
- Sponsor an Event
- Distribute Flyers
- Advertise Outdoors

How to Use AliExpress to Dropship

Now that you have your store filled with products and your first sale made, here is what you need to do.

Dropshipping with AliExpress works similarly to any regular dropshipper. When you receive an order, purchase the item on AliExpress and enter your customer's name and shipping address. The AliExpress seller handles the rest.

It might be a good idea to have a spreadsheet handy with a list of all the products on your site, the amount you're selling them for, the amount they cost on AliExpress and a link to the AliExpress listing. This way, whenever you get an order, it will be easier for you to find the supplier on AliExpress as well as keep track of price changes. You can use Oberlo which can handle all this for you, including making it easier for you to purchase orders on AliExpress and watch for price changes.

When ordering on AliExpress, it's a good idea to let the seller know you're dropshipping. This way, the supplier won't include any invoices or promotions in the package being sent to your customer.

On checkout, you can leave a message for the seller. I recommend leaving a message such as: "We're dropshipping. No promotions & invoices, please!"

2 Commas In 2 Years

Depending on your seller's processing time, you'll receive an email shortly letting you know that your order has been shipped.

Mens Watches Top Brand Luxury GUANQIN Men Sport Tourbillon Automatic Mechanical Leather Wristwatch Moon Phase relogio masculino

Color: Gold Black 🕰️

Leave a message for this seller:

We're dropshipping. No promotions & invoices, please!

AliExpress

My Orders

Payment successfully made

Payment for Order no. 804015██████ has been accepted.

Currently, your payment is 'Being Verified'. Payments are usually verified within 24 hours. After supplier will begin to process your order.
During this time, you are unable to do any operation on your order.

Create an account on Aliexpress
to track your orders online, save your shipping and billing information, and more!

Click the link in the email to view the order, which will allow you to see the tracking number for the order.

Next, head over to your Shopify admin and fulfil that order. Be sure to enter the tracking number, too. Now it's just a matter of waiting for your customers to receive their order. When the order arrives, AliExpress will send you an email asking for confirmation that the order was received. Give some time for the customer to get back to you in case there are any problems with their order. This way, you can bring up the issue with the supplier through AliExpress for them to correct it.

Refunds and Returns

Many AliExpress suppliers don't offer returns. This means you'll have to handle returns and refunds in one of a few ways. When there's an issue with an order, a customer placed on your store, it's usually because the order never arrives or your customer is not happy with their purchase.

For the first case, an order never arriving should be brought up with the AliExpress supplier. In this situation, contact the supplier to resolve the issue or use AliExpress' Buyer Protection.

If your customer is simply not happy with the product, I suggest providing a refund. If the product is damaged, ask your customer to take photos and send those photos to the AliExpress seller and go from there.

Growing Your Dropshipping Business

Once you've made your first few sales, it's time to start looking at how you can grow your dropshipping business.

Eventually you'll begin to figure out who the reliable and quality suppliers are, and those you should stay away from. You should consider building relationships with the reliable ones. This will allow you to get better prices and priority order processing.

I've found most of the suppliers on AliExpress use Skype. If you see yourself frequently ordering from the same seller, it's a good idea to ask them for their Skype username to develop a business relationship. Once you've demonstrated you can bring in recurring sales, some sellers will allow you to place your logo on products, include custom invoices or branded inserts into shipping packages.

2 Commas In 2 Years

Selling a Program / eBook

"Either write something worth reading or do something worth writing about." – Benjamin Franklin.

Programs

Let's start with creating your program:

1. Either learn to code yourself or hire a coder (I suggest looking for coders on freelance sites/forums since they are usually much cheaper and easier to negotiate with compared to people/businesses with websites. If you are dealing with individuals that they may scam, so always use a middleman and/or check the reputation of your coder to ensure he is an expert).

Now you may be thinking what products can I sell? Here are a few suggestions that are in demand, ask your coder what they have already coded for more ideas (note this depends on where and who you are selling to):

- Email Marketers
- Social Media Bots
- SEO Analysis Tools
- Feedback Analysis Tools
- Proxy Scrapers
- Account Recovery Tools
- Mobile Apps / Games

There are thousands of things to sell, just find a forum or create a website you wish to sell on. Let's take the first example of an email marketer:

1. Your first step is to Google 'Programming Forums' and browse through to find one that looks good, where someone will code your email marketer for you (for this example, it shouldn't cost over $100-300 for this to be coded with lifetime updates).

2. Next, you want to find some forums where people would buy this product. For this example, we will need to find some marketing/business forums where there is a marketplace. I Googled 'marketing forums', and found two websites which I wish to target: WebMasterSun and Warrior Forum.

3. Before you even try to sell on a forum, you must build a reputation (which will take time) and connections with trusted members. To do this successfully, I suggest you give back a lot to the community and create smaller groups (on Skype/ Twitter etc.) where you discuss business.

4. Once you have established a name for yourself, get a good graphic designer to create a thread design for your outlining all your features and benefits.

5. You are now ready to put your program up for sale and have your highly reputable friends to 'vouch' for you.

6. If you would like to take it one step further, I suggest creating a website (if you do not know HTML & CSS and do not wish to pay a web developer) on a templated site such as WordPress or Squarespace.

7. Your next step would be creating Facebook Ads, promoting yourself on social media and connecting with others providing them with the chance of affiliate marketing.

8. Once you see sales have plateaued, simply sell your program rights on (this should be around the same price you purchased it for, getting your start-up money back, but this depends highly on the amount of sales you got, it can be much more or less).

eBooks

Writing Your eBook

If you do not wish to spend time and money on a program/product, I highly suggest creating an eBook of value you want to sell. Now, I know you are thinking either you are not a good writer or you don't know what to write about. Well, if you don't know what to write, I suggest thinking of what you enjoy and then think of a problem within that field – for example, if you are writing an eBook on productivity, research common mistakes people make and tips to overcome them.

If you do not feel you are a capable author or are too busy to write a detailed book which you can be proud to publish, you can hire someone to write an eBook for you. Purchasing the ownership to content can be done in two ways, purchasing existing content or paying someone to write new content. If you wish to purchase existing content, then I recommend finding a book you like and contacting the owner about purchasing full ownership to it. Make sure you specify what full ownership would include for you if you don't want him to be able to resell it or modify it make sure you specify that. If you wish to pay someone to write new content for you, then you will either need to give them an empty topic or an outline. An empty topic means you're simply giving them the topic you want them to write about and they will have to create an eBook based around this topic from scratch. This is expensive and might not always reflect exactly what you're looking for. It's also difficult to find an author who is willing and capable of doing this properly. The second option would be to provide a selected author or group of authors with a basic or advanced outline of what you want your book to include. Remember the easier it is for the author, the easier it will be on your pocket. If you're looking for someone to write your content (also known as a ghost writer) then check out sites such as freelancer.com or upwork.com

However, this can be extremely expensive and may take weeks to write, or it might even not be how you expected it to turn out like, so you could opt for one of the options below. However, there is an alternative to this; you can purchase Private Label Rights, Master Resale Rights or Resale rights.

"Private Label Rights (PLR) - PLR allows for re-branding, sale in any way you wish and for it to be changed in any way you wish. You are allowed to but your name as the author of the product, but are not allowed to claim any copyright as the product is available to many others also.

Master Resale Rights (MRR) - MRR rights are very similar to PLR products, apart from you are not allowed to change the product in any way or claim authorship over the product. The beauty of MRR products are that they allow for you to resell the product on to your customer with resell rights. This then allows for your customer to sell on the product to their customer. Master Resale Rights products are generally the most popular form of license you will find online.

Resale Rights (RR) - Resale rights allow for the product to be sold on to your customer as is, it cannot be amended. The customer then has no rights to pass it on or sell to their customers. In basic terms, once you receive a product with resell rights you can sell it on to your customer and the sales stop there.

Giveaway Rights - You can give the product away for free (in any way you wish, unless the license terms state otherwise). You cannot resell or change in any way. These products will usually only include an eBook with no other items. These are good for getting a good reputation in your forum of choice as mentioned earlier."

Go View SEO Secrets Uncovered Ebook

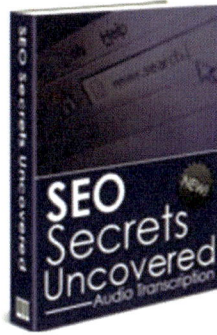

$4.95 To Download

Add to Cart

P.S By placing your order today, you'll also receive the complete transcription to the SEO Secrets Uncovered audio product as a bonus from us, absolutely free!

No More 9 to 5

Today's Lower Price: $5.09
Our Wholesale Price: $5.99
You Save: $0.90
Product ID : 5647979234

Like ‹ 0

Tweet G+1 0

Pin it Bookmark this on Delicious

E-mail to a friend | Add To Wish List

Quantity   1

Add to Cart

Description   Similar PLR eBooks & Resources

- Download File Size - 15,734Kb
- eBook Format - PDF, DOC (source)
- Reading Requirements - Any PDF reader
- Number of Pages 13
- Release Date - 2012
- Suggested Retail Price - $17.00

Reseller Tools

- Includes Sales Page - No
- Includes Download Page - No
- Other Included Pages - Squeeze Page
- Notable Reseller Extras - PSD Graphics (source), Promo Emails (7), Keywords List

Distribution Rights

- Resale Rights - Yes
- Master Resale Rights - No
- Private Label Rights (PLR) - Yes (non-transferrable)
- Giveaway Rights - Yes
- Offered as a Bonus - Yes
- Full Product Copyrights - Yes
- Full Graphic Copyrights - No
- May Modify Product - Yes
- Packaged with Other Products - Yes
- Added to Paid Membership Websites - Yes
- Added to Free Membership Websites - Yes
- May Publish Offline - Yes
- May Sell on Auction Websites - No

Above are some examples of PLR / MRR eBooks you could buy and sell. As you can see "No More 9 to 5" is an MRR eBook that can be

bought for under $6 and has a suggested retail price of $17.00, which is a very nice markup (you could even sell it for more if you want to).

How to Sell Anything

Before we go any further, I want to share with you some of the ways you can sell anything. I was unsure on if I should include this section in my book, since it is so powerful it can be used for evil (making people buy something they shouldn't). However, I decided to share this since there are more good people in the world than bad.

Angle your eBook like a "magic pill". What I mean by this is that people only buy something that gives the end result with no work in between. People buy what they want, not what they need.

A major reason why people buy is scarcity and fear. Here are 3 things people fear:

- Lower status.
- Lack of security.
- Future pain.

This is why some of the worst products (and best) are marketed using the idea of fear and the magic pill. Let's take the multi-billion-pound industry of skincare and anti-ageing cream.

- Anti-ageing cream is marketed as a 'magic pill' type product – stay young without doing anything.
- People buy it to prevent future pain and lower status.

As you can see this can be used for good (such as insurance) or evil (pyramid schemes). Please, please, please, only use this for good. If you wouldn't sell it to family, don't sell it at all. If you are not willing to pressure someone into buying your product, you don't believe in it.

"How you make your money is more important than how much you make." – Gary Vaynerchuk.

Selling Your eBook

Now that you have your eBook ready; you will need to get the graphics completed. The type of graphics required depends on if you are using a sales thread (a dedicated thread or post to your product, this would be found in a forum typically rather than on a website) or a sales page (a dedicated page on a website specifically for your product). Look and find that perfect designer on freelance sites to make your GFX.

Why would someone buy your eBook?

_____
_____

Name 3 ways you will improve your book?

_____
_____
_____

You will also need to decide on the pricing of your product or eBook depending on competitor's prices, your niche and how you want to present your product and if you want multiple packages.

Who is your target market?

_____

How much would you be prepared to pay for your eBook?

_____

Is your eBook so irresistible that it does not need to be sold? _____

Where do you plan on selling your eBook?

_____
_____
_____

So, everything should now be done and ready for release. I would suggest using an autobuy system to ensure you are making money in your sleep and your customers instantly receive what they pay for (I suggest you accept as many payment types as possible, from PayPal to debit cards to bitcoin).

Here are some autobuy websites:
- Gumroad
- FetchApp
- Intubus
- Sellfy
- Pulley
- Simple Goods
- Send Owl
- Selz
- Digital Goods Store
- DPD
- Hex Pay

I suggest you establish yourself in a closed community. A great way to get started out in a fresh market is offering free content, you don't want to make your buyers expect only free content but the perfect balance of free and paid is an unbeatable combination. Just because you're offering something free does not mean it can be junk. Your free content you offer should be better than the paid content that your competition is selling. If you're teaching someone how to cook in your eBook offer a free recipe if users subscribe to your mailing list (see email marketing chapter).

Now your eBook is completely ready for purchase, simply follow the same advice as if your product was a program.

Another place where you could sell your eBooks is on Amazon/ Kindle store. Let's take this example:

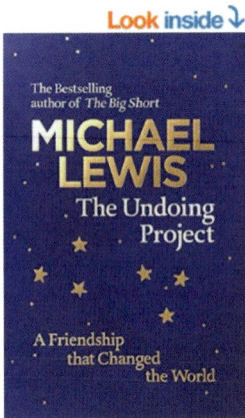

Look inside ↓

The Undoing Project: A Friendship that Changed the World Kindle Edition

by Michael Lewis ▾ (Author)

★★★★☆ ▾   35 customer reviews

▸ See all 4 formats and editions

Kindle Edition	Hardcover
£12.99	£17.00
Read with Our **Free App**	32 Used from £8.62
	44 New from £8.63

Amazon Bestsellers Rank: #1,300 Paid in Kindle Store (See Top 100 Paid in Kindle Store)

#1 in Kindle Store > Books > Business & Finance > **Economics**

#2 in Kindle Store > Books > Business & Finance > **Marketing & Sales**

#2 in Kindle Store > Books > Nonfiction > Science & Maths > **Behavioural Sciences**

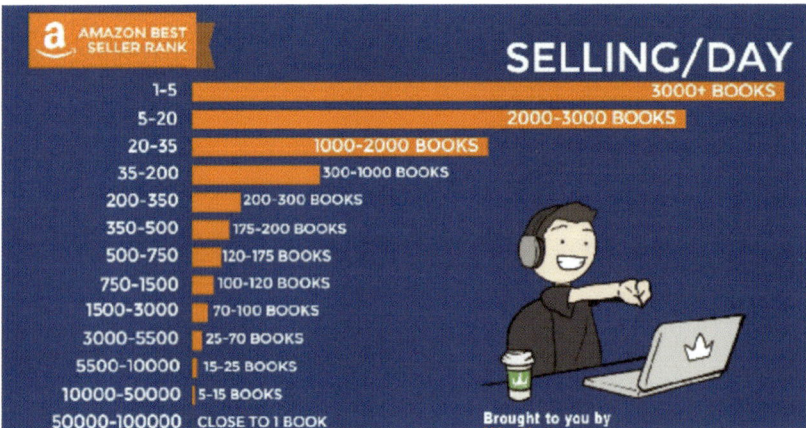

As you can see that author is bringing in hundreds of pounds per day just from that eBook. The power of this is having multiple eBooks for sale. Once you have finished your eBooks, it acts as passive income since little work is required to maintain. Add eBooks as an extra stream of passive income while you focus on the other methods that require more time in this book.

Starting an Agency

"Marketing is the contest for people's attention." – Seth Godin.

Starting an Agency

In this section, I will go into detail on specifically how you can create a successful agency in the digital marketing field (this can easily be transferred to anything such as programming, SEO, graphics and so forth). I will focus on how to build your agency and land clients rather than tips for executing your businesses service (such as SEO and increasing social media exposure). This is because I have looked and found unlimited free resources on Google on how to build a bigger social media / running paid ads and SEO yet hardly anything about practical methods to creating an agency and landing clients to pay you £1000-10000 a month.

Naming Your Company

The first step to creating your agency is thinking of a name for your business. Here are some tips for naming your business:

1. Do not name your business after yourself, it will make it harder to sell in the future.
2. In your company name you might want to have the benefit for your customer. Make your name niche specific.
3. Consider if your company name has been taken (look this up on google, namecheap, and social media platforms).
4. Check on Companies House if your business has already been registered (or its equivalent in the US).
5. Pick a name you would like in 5 years.

Forming Your Company

The next thing I suggest you do is register your company as a LTD or LLC company (depending on your country). A good website for people in the UK that want to register their business legally is Rocket Lawyer and in the US, LegalZoom. You do not always need to register your business, but I suggest this as it can help greatly if someone attempts to sue you. You can always seek for a lawyer to understand more about your country and business. If you are struck for money you can pay lawyers by the hour or you can offer your digital marketing services in return for their services.

You can register your business as something else under a 'DBA' as the name the public will see is whatever you decided e.g. 'Digital Marketing Agency'. For example, register your LTD / LLC with your initials followed by holdings or ventures. E.g. for me it would be 'N.I Holdings' and I would have different DBA's for my business. For example, I would be doing business as 'nMedia Digital Marketing' if that was my agencies name, which is also what your customers would see.

Picking Your Domain

You will need to pick a domain, I suggest the website namecheap which is my personal favorite (or on whatever platform you built your website on). Here are some tips for choosing a domain:
Pick a domain which will be easy to rank to the first page of google.
- Try to make it as simple and self-explanatory as possible.
- Make sure your words are not ambiguous. For example, 'dear' and 'deer' sound the same but are spelt differently.
- Pick a universal domain ending such as .com or .co.uk.

Create Your Website

Your next stop is to create a website where you can showcase your company and work. If you have no previous programing skills in HTML, CSS, PHP or Java, do not worry, you don't always need to code it from scratch or hire someone. You can use a website with templates to create your website; I suggest using Squarespace for a general website and Shopify for eCommerce. It is extremely easy to get the hang of and create a simple yet beautiful website. If you want to learn more about this, you can google or YouTube how to optimize your site. Your website will act as your ultimate employee, it works 24 hours a day, 365 days a year.

I suggest you audit your own website. Here are some great tools for auditing your website for free:

- Nibbler
- PageScoring
- GTMetrix
- Pingdom
- SortSite
- W3C Validation Tool
- Wave Accessibility Tool
- Web Page Test
- SEO Web Page Analyzer
- Check My Colors

Telling Your Story

You must be able to show your brand storytelling both when pitching and when you have a client. You must be able to tell a story for your customers, have a beginning (a hook), a middle (plot) and an end (resolution).

Let's take the example of how a plastic surgeon can implement a good story on their website or social media:

1. **The Hook**, let's start with a shocking fact – "70% of people are insecure about their nose."

2. **The Plot**, now we have someone's attention we need to make it relatable by creating a story with real people – "Susan was one of these people and she seeked our services and within 3 months, her entire life changed, she saw a change in her confidence and was finally able to work up the courage to pursue her dreams."

3. **The Resolution**, get the reader to take action – Put a form asking what users biggest insecurity is and they should enter their email etc. Make sure to end it on a call to action.

That is just a simple example and you need to make sure your story is congruent on all platforms, e.g. website, Twitter, Instagram etc.

The Irrefutable Offer

I'm going to make him an offer he can't refuse.
– The Godfather

The best way in to land a client is to show what you can do upfront. This is because people believe what they see not what they hear. You would do this by emailing / phoning a business cold providing them an offer they cannot refuse.

An 'irrefutably offer' is providing value at first without the expectation of receiving something in return. For example, you would phone up a local business and make them the irrefutable offer that "For completely free, I will rank you to the top of google for a keyword of your choice along with an audit on your digital marketing. Is seeing an increasing in website traffic for free something you would be interested in?" As you can see, it is very hard to decline this offer since there is no catch, what you hope to do by providing a free service such as this is to show your potential client that you are an expert and can increase their revenue, through digital media marketing. In all honesty, when you are starting out, you could even offer to run some businesses social media accounts free for a week to gain experience and as a trial. If you do a good job, there is no reason why a business would not start to pay you once they see an increase in their revenue due to your marketing strategies. Here is one process you can follow during your call:

1. Introduction.
2. Reason/Big Claim.
3. Qualify/Fact Find.
4. Give Value.
5. Close.

Here is an example of what you could use as a checklist for your business audits.

Evaluate your potential client's website
1. Does it load slowly?
2. Does it look aesthetically appealing?
3. Is their content compelling?
4. Do they have video content?
5. Are their "Call to Actions" clear?
6. Is their website mobile-friendly?
7. Does it load slowly on mobile?
8. Does it look aesthetically appealing on mobile?
9. Is their website's sales-funnel easy to follow? In other words, is it simple for their customers to purchase on their website?
10. Can you purchase / contact within 3 clicks?

Evaluate your potential client's Social Media Channels

1. How often are they posting new content?
2. Is their content compelling?
3. You can measure this by the amount of engagement they get on their posts; i.e. High number of likes, comments, shares, reposts, etc. Which posts get the highest engagement:
4. This will help identify their customers' interests so your future posts can cater to their customers and grow their following.
5. Is their content consistent with their brand?
6. Do they offer discounts to their customers if they post about their business?

The irrefutable offer is great for those who want to gain experience, do not have many customers and that are not comfortable with hard selling. Although I still suggest you understand sales and have responses to common objections you will get. This is a numbers game, so get used to rejection and your time wasted – until you get to the point where businesses approach you.

Alternative Methods to Landing Clients

1. **Create a Business Alliance** - create a networking group consisting of 3-5 other people who also sell to the local businesses (or niche) that you target. For example, if you sell social media marketing management to restaurants, partner up with the person who handles their payroll, their payment processing, their insurance, their wine salesperson, etc. Offer 10% commission to anyone who refers a new customer with you – and pay them residually 10% on every monthly payment because they will help retain your customer as well. Once you land businesses, you could even offer discounts if they refer any other businesses that would benefit from your services.

2. **LinkedIn Outreach** - connect with business owners on LinkedIn by being valuable first. If no one can refer you, I suggest you use the irrefutable offer we talked about prior. Build the relationship, share an article or a post or a blog that you wrote with them. Once you add value and they will see you as someone who they can trust and work with, not just someone using their connection as a gateway to solicit them.

3. **Google My Business Listing Unclaimed** - any business that has not claimed their listing on Google is missing out on a huge number of customers and so can be easy sales. You can find businesses who have not yet claimed their listings by entering the following structured search term into Google:

   Search Google for:
   site:plus.google.com "Is this your business?"
   site:plus.google.com "manage this page"

   Or, combine them:
   site:plus.google.com "Is this your business?" "manage this page"

You can also add a specific location to the search at the end of the term, and even a niche.

4. **Yelp.com** - This strategy is particularly useful if you sell to restaurants, salons and other businesses people tend to search for using Yelp.com. Here's the Yelp search strategy to find qualified prospects:

   Go to Google.com and do a search exactly like this (substitute location or business type): site:yelp.com "watch video" + restaurant + London

   This will pull up Yelp listings in Google of businesses that feature of Video on their Yelp listing/profile.

   Having a video on your profile costs money, and often costs at a minimum £300/mo. to have an updated Yelp listing (on up to £1500+/mo. depending on the type of advertising package they've purchased from Yelp). What does this tell you about them? They are a qualified prospect because they are already paying for local marketing and advertising.

Pricing

The pricing is up to you, and you can work your way up after working for free to show what you can do; however, these are the prices I would charge per month, if I were just starting out. Note that these prices depend on the size of the business and many other factors. Here are some pricing and packages you could use.

Website Package (£749)

- Create a website.
- Includes domain and server cost.

Social Media Package (£749)

- Twitter.
- Facebook fan page.
- Instagram.
- Snapchat.
- Pinterest.
- YouTube.
- Email Marketing.
- Blog Posts to increase SEO.

Alternative Package (£749)

- Professionally filmed "about us" video.
- Logo created.
- Business makeover.
- Business cards created.
- Business photoshoot.

Advertising Package (£749)

- Website Marketing Funnel.
- Increase SEO ranking.
- Google AdWords.
- Facebook Ads.
- Email List.

Make sure to tell the business that "Paid traffic will be at the business owner's cost".

All Inclusive (£1999)

- Social Media Package
- Alternative Package
- Advertising Package

Once you show value to your clients and increased revenue, you can start to charge higher amounts. You can begin charging each client £2000-10000+ a month, once you have established a good reputation and track record of increasing the businesses profits.

I also suggest you include a:

- Cancel anytime policy with a 30-day notice, for both parties.

- 100% money-back guarantee refund policy, for your services.

Niche

When starting out, I suggest taking everything on seeing what you are good and bad at. If you are passionate about something, even better, target them. Here is a list of some niches you could choose.

- Cosmetic Surgeons
- Dermatologists
- Tanning salons
- Chiropractors
- Dentists
- Gyms
- Personal Trainers
- Car dealers
- Motorcycle dealers
- Auto Financing / Mortgage Financing
- Auto Repair / Body Shops
- Car Rental
- Window Tinting
- Divorce Lawyers
- Personal Injury
- Estate Planning
- Florists
- Catering Companies
- Photographers & Videographers
- DJs
- Wedding or Wedding Planners
- Limousine Drivers
- Personal Chefs
- Health and beauty market
- Hair salons
- Nail salons
- Day spas
- Construction/Home Services
- AC/Heating
- Handyman
- Heating And Cooling
- Housekeeping/ Maid Services
- Painters
- Plumbers
- Bathroom Remodeling
- Pest Control
- Carpet Cleaning
- Decks & Porches
- Pools & Spas
- Roofing
- Fencing
- Landscaping
- Siding
- Flooring
- Locksmiths
- Glass repair
- Security Systems
- Interior Designers
- Home Theater
- Child care
- Veterinarians
- Pet groomers
- Tattoo shops
- Martial Arts Gyms
- Yoga
- Pilates Business Formation
- Auto Insurance
- Life Insurance
- Health Insurance
- Dental Insurance
- Annuities
- Wealth managements
- Accountants/CPA
- Financial Planners
- Consultants
- HR Specialists
- Real Estate
- Home Inspectors
- Home Appraisers
- Real Estate Investors
- Foreclosure/Short Sale Experts
- Moving Companies
- Event Planners
- Weight loss specialists
- Dieticians
- Massage Therapists
- Education
- Private schools
- Technical training centers (i.e. Wielding, Vocational Training)
- Travel Agents
- Resorts
- Timeshares

Example

If I had to start an agency helping local businesses from scratch, I would begin by handing out flyers/business cards or cold calling businesses. I would begin by thinking of local businesses or googling businesses in your local area (which are not franchised). Let's take this business for an example.

Pauls Reptile Den, For all your Reptile needs,
paulsreptileden.com/ ▾
Welcome to Paul's **Reptile** Den I am an independent retailer of **reptiles** and **reptile** related Products. I have over 34 years ... Online **Shop** ... Paul's **Reptile** Den run by myself Paul is situated on Barnet Road, **Potters** Bars. We have been ...

What I would do next is quickly scan through his website to see what the business does and if they are qualified to pitch to.

The next step would be to find the phone number of this independent retailer on their website and cold call them offering your irrefutable offer. In this example, I phoned the owner and pitched, giving them my irrefutable offer to get my foot in the door and prove how I can increase the businesses revenue. Although this was one of the worst pitches I have ever given, the owner could not refuse thanks to our irrefutable offer.

I then ranked the business to the top of Google for his chosen keyword through using a PBN link (very basic SEO).

My next step was to complete the free business audit. For this example, I firstly completed a check on SEMrush.com to check his traffic and SEO followed by a speedtest for his website using Google developers 'Page Insights'.

2 Commas In 2 Years

17 / 100 Suggestions Summary

! **Should Fix:**

Optimize images

Properly formatting and compressing images can save many bytes of data.

Optimize the following images to reduce their size by 1.6MiB (52% reduction).

Compressing http://paulsreptileden.com/wp-content/uploads/2014/01/slide_2.jpg could save 343.2KiB (80% reduction).

Domain Overview "paulsreptileden.com" ⓘ

● ORGANIC SEARCH		● PAID SEARCH		● BACKLINKS	
92 +28% TRAFFIC		**0** 0% TRAFFIC		**212** TOTAL BACKLINKS	
SEMrush Rank	979K	Keywords	0	Referring Domains	
Keywords	286 +3%	Traffic Cost	$0	Referring IPs	
Traffic Cost	$37 +147%				

I then followed through the checklist I included earlier, evaluating his website and social media channels.

After evaluating his digital marketing, I followed up with an email stating everything I believe was good and what could be improved (which is where my paid services would come in).

From   Neema Imantabari <neema@neemaimantabari.com> ▾

To   info@paulsreptileden.com ×   CC BCC

Reply
to

Subject   Free Business Audit & SEO

Attachments ▾   Signatures ▾ Options ▾

B *I*   ≔ ⋮≣ ⧈ ⧉ Formats ▾ Font Family   ▾ Font Sizes   ▾   A ▾ A ▾   ⸆ 🖼

Hi Paul,

I contacted you on Friday about a free business audit and SEO ranking service for a keyword (Reptile Den) which I have completed.

Evaluation for your digital marketing:

Positives

-You have a nice looking, easily navigable and responsive website that looks good on both desktop and mobile.

-You have a Facebook, Instagram, Twitter, Youtube account.

-eCommerce is enabled for online sales & good range of products.

-You have avoided landing page redirects.

-SEO is good. 284 top keywords to help SEO with 210 backlinks.

To Improve

- Your website can load much quicker (20 critical errors on your website for this.)

- Your social media content is not always compelling and with no call to actions.

- Social media channels are very hard to find, no link on website

- Consistent posts on social media are not there.

-Snapchat, YouTube, and Twitter are non-existent / very inactive.

-Copywriting can be improved.

-Not much traffic (90 in your best month).

-No paid Ad's running.

I will contact you on Monday via phone, giving you the opportunity to increase your revenue if we are a good fit for future business. Have a wonderful day!

Neema Imantabari.

This example went as well as it could have. After calling him on Monday, I showed Paul how he was ranked to the top of Google and the value of digital marketing. We later scheduled a face to face meeting, to finalise the details for the paid service I was going to provide.

That's all the information you need to land a client. If you are going to go out and do this, you will need to read and study the following or / and outsource these:

- Google AD Words
- Facebook / Instagram Ads
- Search Engine Optimisation
- How to run a successful email campaign
- How to successfully use social media for businesses.

Please also read the social media section in this book, which you may find useful for this. You can read up on these in detail on books, articles online and videos on YouTube, you do not want unhappy customers. You must study and read a lot of books / videos purely on social media since this is not the focus of my book. There are thousands of free resources on how to increase your social media coverage, and that is why I have not covered that in this book. I do not recommend buying any courses, since all information can be found for free.

If you are in a rush to make money immediately and whilst you are taking the time to learn everything yourself, you can outsource this to people on Upwork after you land a client, although you will not have a huge net profit.

<u>Tips</u>

- Advertising your services online. Look at thumbtack.com.
- Ensure you build up a decent network before you promote your services, don't create a social media marketing agency with 20 followers, practice what you preach.
- You can create leaflets and business cards online on websites such as canva.com.
- You will need a contract – you can create one on LawDepot or Rocket Lawyer.
- Read through the social media and email marketing section.

<u>Hard Selling</u>

In this section, I will cover closes and rebuttals, to help you close the deal. The first thing you need to know is how to differentiate between a complaint and an objection. An objection is a reason why a prospect cannot buy, rather than a complaint which is a reason they won't.

- An example of objection – I am not the decision maker.
- An example of complaint – The price is too high.

The way you will handle the response depends on if it is an objection or a complaint. If it is a complaint, stay sold and eventually they will get sold. But remember, you need to balance this with love and empathy, people don't like being sold to.

<u>Rebuttals</u>

I don't have the time - *"I understand you don't have a lot of time now, providing I can show you how you can increase your revenue for free, could you spare me three minutes?"*

I already have someone running my digital marketing - *"I understand that you already have someone that runs your digital marketing. But there is a difference between how Ronaldo and I play football. Your digital marketer is an amateur, and I am a professional. He costs you money; I make you money, that's the difference."*

The price is too high - *"I understand why you might think the price is too high. You would only buy when value exceeds the value of your money. That's why I'm providing a service that will increase your revenue by that of which you paid me, or I will refund the difference."*

The price is too high - *"I understand why you might think the price is too high, in fact, the majority of our loyal clients thought this initially. Let's do this."*

I need to think about it - *"I agree with you; you do need to think about it. But try this, think of a book. Get the picture? You see, thought is instantaneous. I need you to make a decision now. Do or don't, either is fine for me, but I need know."*

I need to talk to my Spouse/business partner - *"I completely agree with you, if your wife is anything like my girlfriend, we talk about anything. But when she knows I have a great deal waiting, she wouldn't stop me from making an investment in the family that felt good. Besides, it's better to ask for forgiveness than permission. Let's do this."*

I don't have the money - *"I understand you do not currently have the money. What local lenders could you speak to while we figure out a payment plan and tailor a package to your needs?"*

I want your best price - *"I understand you want my best price, but the listed price is my best for the high service I am providing. We could choose a different package if that would suit you better."*

Closes

"I only want you to test me out, try £500 for just the first month so I can show you the value of my service. If you see no value, no harm, we cancel it and I provide you with a full refund. You won't be out in front of the store with a coffee cup in your hand, let's do this."

"If you wrote me a check for £1000 and I returned £2000, would you do the deal. Well, that is exactly what I'm doing for you. I'm here to serve you, not sell to you. Let's make some money together. When do you want me to start?"

"It is a lot of money, but there is no shortage of money on this planet – only a shortage of successful businesses providing a great service like yours. I am here to help you. Let's do this."

"Okay, I have space for one more client. I will start your service at the beginning of the month."

"How could you justify and investment of this size?" – This question allows for people who just need that little push to justify why this is a worthwhile investment, the role will be reversed, they will try to sell to you.

Closing Tips

- Take a nice pen with you, with the correct paperwork when meeting someone face-to-face.
- Get your client to saying "yes, yes, yes" early on. They will be much more likely to say yes to whatever you say next.
- Use the "Sullivan Nod" when closing a deal. Nod 3 times slightly up and down during whatever it is you want them to agree on.
- Always remain seated when negotiating and closing.
- Always present your proposal in writing.
- Always agree and stay positive with the buyer, no matter the response, objection – know you can find a solution and come to an agreement.

Secrets to Coming up With Business Ideas

"You get paid in direct proportion to the difficult of the problems you solve." – Elon Musk.

Look at Other Successful Businesses Ideas

Focus on seeing what already works in the marketplace; this proves that there is a demand for your product. See the ideas other businesses are using and improve on them, instead of trying to make an entirely new product in a market which you know nothing about. Focus on an existing product and master marketing, sales and the execution of the idea.

1. Find a good idea.
2. Improve it as well as you can.
3. Executing the idea really well.

Nearly no profitable business was the first of its kind; Apple was not the first company to come out with personal computers, Facebook was not the first social networking site, McDonald's was not the first fast food business, the list is endless. Your ideas are worthless until you execute them.

AWFUL IDEA = -1
WEAK IDEA = 1
SO-SO IDEA = 5
GOOD IDEA = 10
GREAT IDEA = 15
BRILLIANT IDEA = 20

NO EXECUTION = $1
WEAK EXECUTION = $1000
SO-SO EXECUTION = $10,000
GOOD EXECUTION = $100,000
GREAT EXECUTION = $1,000,000
BRILLIANT EXECUTION = $10,000,000

TO MAKE A BUSINESS, YOU NEED TO MULTIPLY THE TWO. THE MOST
BRILLIANT IDEA, WITH NO EXECUTION, IS WORTH $20. THE MOST BRILLIANT
IDEA TAKES GREAT EXECUTION TO BE WORTH $20,000,000.

This is relatively easy with medium risk. However, there is a limit to the amount you will make since the market is already extremely saturated, you will have to execute so much better if you want to get significant market share.

Look at What's Working in Other Spaces and Bring it to Your Space

See what other successful companies are doing in a bigger market and bring the same idea to your niche. For example, look at a successful company such as Airbnb and transfer the concept to a smaller niche such as renting cars. A successful example of this would-be Instagram; they saw how effectively Facebook was operating and decided to pick a niche within Facebook's audience, photographers. They focused on marketing it as a photographer's app, and eventually, Facebook ended up buying Instagram for $1 Billion and made it mainstream. The reason this works is that you can cater to a smaller niche, while Facebook was looking to please everyone, Instagram focused on a smaller group of people, and they wanted to ensure that they brought it into a new space. This concept works whether you are bringing something to a similar market or an entirely different one.

Creating a New Product or Service

Another way you can create a new product or service is to see if there is a problem that needs to be fixed.

You can reverse engineer the demand of the marketplace. Pay attention to what people care about and build goods or services around that. For example, everyone no matter their income level cares about their time since it is so scarce. This means that if you create products or services that save time, you can create a good idea that you know there is a demand for. Once you understand the principle of inversion and supply and demand you can create a product you know, there is a demand for, through reverse engineering. Think like about your audience, what would they buy and why? For example, a reason why audiobooks since release have become hugely popular in recent times is that it saves time, as people can listen faster than they can read, allowing them to absorb the information quicker and even complete other tasks while listening.

This has a high risk since if you create a product and do not correctly patent it (even if you do), competitors may see how good your idea is and they can just copy your idea. Like I mentioned earlier, people who know how to execute will simply get VC funding and launch the product quickly. Thus, I would personally only suggest this method to entrepreneurs with experience and can get funding. This is due to the fact if you do not blow up quickly, competitors will dominate you (e.g. Mark Zuckerberg who allegedly stole the Winklevoss brother's idea). I suggest you get great at executing and hire a great team before you do this.

Trend Stacking

A great method to coming up with ideas is called trend stacking. This is where you choose multiple trends when creating a brand-new product. For example, when Snapchat was being made, Evan Spiegel stacked multiple trends. These being social networking, apps, selfies and privacy. He chose enough trends to make it successful, without picking too which would mean his product would not be able to reach a mass market. By picking multiple good trends, he was able to appeal to a niche, without making the market too small.

Compete with Giants

The final suggestion is to find a huge company that is doing something inefficiently and undercut them. For example, Uber undercut the Taxi business whereby they added more value to all parties involved. An example of a way you could undercut Uber right now is to charge a lower fee than they do (although this wouldn't be very profitable). What would happen next is that once you acquire a certain market share and reputation, the huge business will not be able to compete with (both in terms of price and features) and therefore would have to buy you out (or another big business within that niche.)

I am currently using this concept with my main business, where we are trying to transform the internet security industry, by destroying the likes of Norton, Avira and MacAfee. As we do not believe anti-viruses are secure in the slightest. Without getting into it in detail, we are creating something that renders anti-virus solutions useless, meaning a company such as McAfee would have to buy us out if they want to remain competitive within the internet security industry.

This is also risky but potentially the most rewarding of these methods, you can also use this in conjunction with the other methods.

Final Words

Congratulations for completing this book. Your next step is to choose which methods you want to take action on, if you haven't already.

Start-Up

What item's do you not need that you can sell around the house?

_____

_____

_____

How much did you make from selling unused items on eBay?

_____

Arbitrage

Do you want to flip items?

_____

What items do you want to flip and how much can you buy and sell for?

_____

_____

_____

Providing a Service

Do you wish to provide a service online? _____

What skill do you wish to learn and where do you want to provide your service and for how much?

_____

_____

_____

Outsourcing

Do you wish to use any of the outsourcing methods? If so which ones.

_____

_____

_____

Social Media

Do you plan on building/buying a social media account and monetize it? If so, in what niche? And how do you plan on monetizing it?

_____

_____

_____

Email Marketing

Do you plan on email marketing? _____

What niche do you want your audience to be and what are you going to provide?

_____

_____

_____

eCommerce

Do you plan on creating an eCommerce store? _____

In what niche? _____

What methods do I plan to use to market?

_____

_____

_____

_____

Selling Programs / eBooks

Do you want to sell programs / eBooks? _____

Starting an Agency

Are you going to start an agency? _____

What type of agency? _____

What methods do you plan on using to land clients?

_____

_____

Are you going to outsource the work? If so, where?

_____

I appreciate your time, and wish you the best on your journey. Visit my website Imantabari.com for more valuable information. If you need any help please feel free to send me a message on Imantabari.com/contact.

Be great,

Neema Imantabari.

"Time goes on. So, whatever you're going to do, do it. Do it now. Don't wait." –
Robert De Niro.

Acknowledgements

This book could not have happened without so many people. First and foremost, my wonderful family. I thank you for what you have done, although I might not show it at times - you have provided me with opportunity and showed me the value of hard work. Likewise, a huge thank you to my Aunt and Uncle for helping me register my businesses and accepting payments because of my age.

I thank my friends for the countless laughs and ideas you have given me. You have made many ordinary moments, extraordinary.

After my family and friends, there is an amazing team, without whose incredible work I would not be in the position I am in. A special thank you to Zach Baptiste, for over a year of dedication and input. I would also like to thank my Lawyer, Melanie for helping the technical side of my business, allowing me to focus on what I do best.

For the cover of the book, I am to thank Vikki and Thomas Parry, who helped transform my ideas into reality.

I would like to thank other author's whose words have influenced this book and my businesses. Especially the work of Gary Vaynerchuk and Grant Cardone whose ideas have helped shaped my approach to business.

I'd also like to thank my critics who have taught me to take nothing anyone says personally. If it doesn't matter in the macro, don't let it bother you in the micro.

I thank you all for helping me on my journey.

About the Author

Neema Imantabari is a 17-year-old entrepreneur who has created multiple successful online businesses and income streams. At present, he is the Founder and CEO of a successful digital marketing agency, helping businesses create change and growth within their business.

In Neema's 3 years of internet marketing, he has experimented with almost every method to making money online. Neema's portfolio also includes a network of over 1,000,000 social media followers.

For more information, please see: **Imantabari.com**

Connect with Neema on social media:

@NeemaBusiness

@NeemaBusiness

NeemaImantabari

Printed in Great Britain
by Amazon